Endorsements

"How often do you hear people say, 'I want to be the best version of myself.' Then they don't take the ACTION or find the resilience to do it. In *The Kairos Code,* Josh Kosnick delivers the framework to LIVE IT one day at a time. Get ready to be challenged to TAKE ACTION."

Ben Newman
USA Today TOP 5 Mindset & Performance Coach
2x *Wall Street Journal* Bestselling Author

"This isn't just another leadership book—it's a soulful invitation to cross the bridges that lead to your most integrated self."

Rene Rodriguez
Speaker and *Wall Street Journal* Best Selling Author of
Amplify Your Influence

"Endless wisdom and timeless principles for pursuing your calling and living life by design. *The Kairos Code* is a must-read for anyone who believes they were made for more!"

Jordan Montgomery
CEO at Montgomery Companies
USA Today Bestselling Author of *The Art of Encouragement*

"So many leaders are winning in the marketplace and losing at home. Josh Kosnick gets it—and he wrote the playbook for change. If you're ready to build a life that's both successful and significant, *The Kairos Code* is your guide."

Jon Gordon
Bestselling Author of *The Energy Bus* and *The One Truth*

"*The Kairos Code* isn't just a leadership book—it's a raw, honest journey through pain, purpose, and personal reinvention. Josh Kosnick invites you to confront the resistance in your life and offers a framework that fuses faith, discipline, and legacy into something deeply transformational."

Joe Thomas
NFL Hall of Famer, 10x Pro Bowler

"Some books challenge how you think. Others challenge how you live. *The Kairos Code* does both. This book is for high performers who understand that their worth doesn't come from what they do but from who they are. His vulnerability will inspire any struggling professional to redefine their priorities and reclaim their purpose."

Mark O'Donnell
Visionary, EOS® Worldwide, and

Kelly Knight
Integrator, EOS® Worldwide, Co-authors of *People: Dare to Build an Intentional Culture*

THE KAIROS CODE

*Discover Your Purpose,
Tap into Higher Performance, and
Become a Leader of Eternal Impact*

THE KAIROS CODE

*Discover Your Purpose,
Tap into High Performance, and
Become a Leader of Eternal Impact*

JOSH KOSNICK

THE KAIROS CODE © 2025 by Josh Kosnick. All rights reserved.

Printed in the United States of America
Published by Igniting Souls
PO Box 43, Powell, OH 43065
IgnitingSouls.com

This book contains material protected under international and federal copyright laws and treaties. Any unauthorized reprint or use of this material is prohibited. No part of this book may be reproduced or transmitted in any form or by any means, electronic or mechanical, including photocopying, recording, or by any information storage and retrieval system, without express written permission from the author.

LCCN: 2025911801
Paperback ISBN: 978-1-63680-529-0
Hardback ISBN: 978-1-63680-530-6
eBook ISBN: 978-1-63680-561-0

Available in paperback, hardcover, e-book, and audiobook.

All Scripture quotations, unless otherwise indicated, are taken from the Holy Bible, New International Version®, NIV®. Copyright © 1973, 1978, 1984 by Biblica, Inc.™ Used by permission of Zondervan. All rights reserved worldwide.

Scripture quotations from The ESV® Bible (The Holy Bible, English Standard Version®), © 2001 by Crossway, a publishing ministry of Good News Publishers. Used by permission. All rights reserved.

Any Internet addresses (websites, blogs, etc.) and telephone numbers printed in this book are offered as a resource. They are not intended in any way to be or imply an endorsement by Igniting Souls, nor does Igniting Souls vouch for the content of these sites and numbers for the life of this book.

Some names and identifying details may have been changed to protect the privacy of individuals.

The superscript symbol IP listed throughout this book is known as the unique certification mark created and owned by Instant IP^{IP}. Its use signifies that the corresponding expression (words, phrases, chart, graph, etc.) has been protected by Instant IP^{IP} via smart contract. Instant IP^{IP} is designed with the patented smart contract solution (US Patent: 11,928,748), which creates an immutable time-stamped first layer and fast layer identifying the moment in time an idea is filed on the blockchain. This solution can be used in defending intellectual property protection. Infringing upon the respective intellectual property, i.e., IP, is subject to and punishable in a court of law.

To my family—Jenna, Ella, Harper, Kensington, and Camden,

You are my greatest blessing. You were my light when the world felt dark. You remind me daily of who I am, and more importantly, Whose I am. This book is a testament to God's goodness, the power of grace, and the legacy we are building together—one bridge at a time.

TABLE OF CONTENTS

Foreword by Mark O'Donnell and Kelly Knight . . . xiii
Introduction: The 5 Bridges of Kairos. xv

PART ONE: THE RISE

Chapter 1: Cut From the Same Cloth 3
Chapter 2: Chasing Ghosts, Leading Giants 7
Chapter 3: Breaking the Curse, Carrying the Torch. . . . 13
Chapter 4: Strive to Never Arrive 21
Chapter 5: The Fall. 31
Chapter 6: A Knock at the Door 37
    June 16, 2021 38
Chapter 7: The Power of the Pause 43
Chapter 8: They're Watching. 51
Chapter 9: The Spiritual Awakening. 55
Chapter 10: The New Mission 61
Chapter 11: Hard Reset: How 75 Days of Pain Rewired My Mind, Body, and Vision. 67
Chapter 12: From Idols to Impact 75
    Before We Begin: What's the Gap Between the Life You Have . . . and the Life You're Called to Live? 84

PART TWO: THE 5 BRIDGES OF KAIROS

Chapter 13: The Spiritual Bridge
(The Unconscious Being and Metaphysical) 89
    The Spirit Within. 96
Chapter 14: The How of the Spiritual Bridge 105
    Mentors 105
    Books/Podcasts/Debates 106
    The Word of God.......................107
    Church..............................108
    Bible Study...........................108
Chapter 15: The Internal Bridge
(Mental Health, Physical Health, Intellectual,
and Emotional)............................. 111
    Physical 111
    Mental 124
    Intellectual 127
    Emotional............................130
Chapter 16: The Relationship Bridge 133
    Relationship 1: God 134
    Relationship 2: YOU.....................135
    Relationship 3: Spouse or Significant Other ...140
    Relationship 4: Your Kids 145
    Relationship 5: Other Relationships 158
Chapter 17: The Environment Bridge
(Professional, Financial, Creative, Adventure, Material) 165
    Professional 166
    Financial 168
    Creative 170
    Adventure............................171

Material 173
 Final Word on Environment 174

Chapter 18: The Legacy Bridge
(Personal Growth, Character, Unlived Life) 179
 Ready to Discover What's Really Driving
 Your Life?............................189

Conclusion................................191

Endnotes 195

About the Author 197

FOREWORD

BY MARK O'DONNELL AND KELLY KNIGHT

Some books challenge how you think. Others challenge how you live. *The Kairos Code* does both.

Rather than handing over a list of habits for readers to follow, Josh Kosnick shares his powerful story of hitting rock bottom and then climbing back to the top. He communicates with clarity, insight, and vulnerability that will inspire any struggling professional to redefine their priorities and reclaim their purpose.

This book is for high performers who understand that their worth doesn't come from what they do but from who they are. It speaks to anyone who has built a life that appears successful from the outside but is chaotic within.

Through the 5 Bridges of Kairos[IP], Josh offers you a lifeline to unite your past and your future, allowing you to bring your gifts into the world without burning out in the process. It's about discovering who you really are and leaving behind what doesn't matter as you embrace the life that's waiting for you.

If you're tired of focusing on achievements rather than values, if you're tired of sacrificing your family for your job, if you're tired of living as who you think you should be rather than who you are—this is the book for you.

JOSH KOSNICK

Josh invites you on a journey to discover your legacy. As he says, your legacy isn't what you leave behind but what you invest in those around you.

If you're ready to stop pretending and start living, your first step is here.

Mark O'Donnell
Visionary & CEO at EOS Worldwide

Kelly Knight
President & Integrator at EOS Worldwide

INTRODUCTION

THE 5 BRIDGES OF KAIROS

The ancient Greeks had two words for time: Kairos and Chronos.

Chronos refers to chronological or sequential time. It is better associated with the Gregorian calendar that we live our lives by in modern society.

Kairos, on the other hand, signifies a period or season, a moment of indeterminate time during which a significant event occurs.

Chronos is quantitative and linear in nature.

Kairos is qualitative and permanent in nature.

The ancient Greek definition of Kairos is the right or opportune moment. This word is also used in the New Testament. The Biblical definition is the appointed time in the purpose of God (Mark 1:15). In either sense, it is qualitative time where you move forward in the present, untethered by any moving clock or calendar.

There's a theory out there (and it's just a theory, as it's impossible for us to prove) that God was speaking to both Moses on the top of Mount Sinai and Elijah at the top of Mount Carmel simultaneously, outside the realm of Chronos time. That's how they both knew that the Messiah would come after them and fulfill the prophecy. Why is that significant? Well, beyond the two different mountains and the fact that the two are approximately 250 miles apart in a straight line, Moses and Elijah appeared in the Old Testament 400 years apart.

It is nearly impossible for our minds to comprehend that theory. We've lived our entire lives in Chronos, in a linear timeframe. Furthermore, we are not God. We are neither omnipresent nor transcendent.

But that doesn't mean we cannot catch glimpses of Kairos. I'm on a mission to spread awareness and to create more Kairos time for myself. When you fully embrace Kairos, you stop drawing fine lines of separation between the past, present, and future. Rather than time being sequential and literal, time becomes holistic, flexible, and transformative.

If you're in Kairos, you can tap into higher levels of being, connection, and inspiration.

Chronos time passes whether you're conscious of it or not. For any of us who have raised kids or are currently raising kids, we know that time really flies. One moment, you're holding your new little blessing, and the next moment, you're walking her down the aisle or sending him off to college.

But Kairos time can only be experienced when you're fully absorbed in the moment. It gives a whole new meaning to "be where your feet are." A few moments in Kairos will advance and transform you more than a lifetime of Chronos.

Being "busy" . . . that's Chronos time and thinking.

Advancement in life . . . that's Kairos!

I named my company Kairos Coaching & Consulting because I believe the Moment is NOW!

Right now is the moment we reclaim our lives from the Chronos world we live in.

Right now is the moment we fully claim the gifts that God endowed us with.

Right now is the moment we leave the impact we desire in this world.

Most people think they have all the time in the world. They don't recognize their own mortality, and because of this, they don't chase down their goals with the aggressiveness they should. They defer taking risks, vacations, and saving money for another time because they make the faulty assumption that they have the time.

When I formed Kairos Coaching, I was keenly aware of how many coaches and programs there were out there. I've had at least one coach in my life at any given time for over 20 years. I've invested hundreds of thousands of dollars into my own personal development throughout my career. Some coaches focus on mindset, some on performance, some on physical, some on mental . . . the list goes on.

When I've been at my best, I was firing on all cylinders, meaning my physical and mental health were at peak, my family and relationships were strong, and my professional and financial game were on point. Essentially, I was a whole person with what I call work/life integration . . . There is no such thing as balance!

I endeavored to create a coaching track that tackles this elusive work/life integration most people seek. I set my sights on creating a track that builds Super Humans.

I call it the 5 Bridges of Kairos[IP] . . .

1. Spiritual
2. Internal
3. Relationship
4. Environment
5. Legacy

Some of you are suffering from self-doubt, while others are scared of your full potential. It's my mission to help people reach their full potential so they can lead their unlived lives. Build them into Super Humans!

It's our longing to reclaim who we really are.

—Erwin McManus

We somehow know deep down that we are not living at our human level. Human beings have the highest intention (in the animal kingdom), and we're the only species that can live outside of our intention.

Not understanding this notion is at the core of depression.

You cannot be depressed if you can imagine a different self—a different you, a different life, a different world. Depression, at its core, is that your reality doesn't match the ideals that are haunting you. Despair, depression, and anxiety are, in some ways, beautiful reminders that we're meant for more.

You are both a work of art and an artist at work!
—Erwin McManus

Human genius is natural to who we are. Every human being is extraordinary, but we often die very ordinary. Your highest self is your highest value to others, and your highest value to others is your highest self!

In Steven Pressfield's masterful book, *The War of Art*, he writes about the invisible and insidious force of "resistance."

Pressfield calls out "Resistance's Greatest Hits":

1. The pursuit of any calling
2. The launching of any entrepreneurial venture
3. Any diet or health regimen
4. Any program of spiritual advancement
5. Any activity whose aim is tighter abdominals
6. Any course or activity aimed at overcoming an unwholesome habit or addiction
7. Education of every kind
8. Any act of political, moral, or ethical courage

9. The undertaking of any enterprise or endeavor whose aim is to help others
10. Any act that entails a commitment of the heart
11. The taking of any principled stand in the face of adversity

For fifteen years, I had a tremendous mentor and coach, John Wright Sr., who also shared a passion for this book. He came up with the concept of "The River of Resistance" based on Pressfield's book.

Imagine the Mighty Mississippi with every predator known to freshwater or saltwater.

John labeled five categories that I've expanded on:

The Walrus = Laziness
The Mermaid = Temptations and Addictions
The Crab = Naysayers and Negative Thoughts
The Shark = Fear
The Library = Re-reading negative chapters from
    your past

Those are just the creatures that could hurt you, but there are plenty of other obstacles you would face while fighting against the current of this river. Whirlpools, fallen branches, and hidden rocks threaten to pull you under at every turn. With each stroke, you wonder how you can make it out alive.

Forget the literal river; this is the river of life.

Whirlpools of self-doubt force your head under, and unexpected trials scratch your feet or block your path.

The cuttlefish is the ultimate victim of the ocean. Like a cuttlefish clouds the water with ink and slips away, the victim-player obscures the truth to avoid responsibility and draw sympathy. How often are you avoiding the truth in your life and playing the victim?

The cleaner fish is the people pleaser of the ocean, who always adapts to others' demands. Cleaner fish spend their lives servicing larger fish by removing parasites. In return, they gain protection and food. But sometimes, they clean even when it's unnecessary—or at their own risk—just to stay in the good graces of their "clients." Their entire identity revolves around keeping others happy.

Like the cleaner fish, the people pleaser in each of us hustles to serve everyone else—hoping to be liked, even if it means ignoring our own needs in the process.

Sirens—yes, I know they're mythical, but in real life, they're all too familiar. They're the shiny objects that distract us from reaching our full potential. They sing the song of laziness or instant gratification, pulling you off course and making you forget why you were in the water in the first place.

This is the river of life we live in—fast, dangerous, and demanding.

How you swim in it defines whether or not you can make it to the other side.

Resistance is natural. We will face this river of resistance any time we are attempting to break free from what is deemed as "normal."

The moment is NOW that we learn to navigate the river of resistance in each of our lives.

PART ONE
THE RISE

CHAPTER 1

Cut From the Same Cloth

In early November 2004, I asked for a raise while working as a Sales Manager at Best Buy. I was leading one of the top five Best Buys in the country, and I knew that most others in my position were being paid more than I was simply because they were older than me.

I was young and naïve to the corporate world, a 24-year-old college dropout at the time. I began working retail at 16 years old, when I started selling pagers and cell phones for Circuit City. These weren't the cell phones we carry now; they were the colorless-screened Nokias and Motorolas.

A friend recruited me to Best Buy after I decided to leave school. Things were going well, but my father had always taught me that if I were a top performer who put in the effort, I would earn more. I carried that methodology with me when I asked for the raise. I showed my track record of success, the long hours I'd been putting in on the weekends, and the training and development of the sales staff.

Despite all of that, the answer was "NO"!

The Store Manager told me my trajectory and path were great. I would soon be offered opportunities to be a Store Manager, and if I did well there, I would be offered a District position.

The problem, I'm a very impatient person by nature. I also didn't like that at every position, there was a cap on my earnings. A ladder to climb, but with a ceiling just above every rung.

Two days after I was told NO for a raise, a call came in. A financial advisor was trying to schedule me for a meeting. At 24 years old, I spent most of my money on my bills, partying on the weekends, and unnecessary purchases from Best Buy.

I was not an ideal target client for this advisor!

As I listened to his pitch, he told me what company he was with, and then my mind started to race. This young and ambitious advisor happened to work for my dad.

I stopped him mid-sentence: "I don't want this to come off arrogant, but do you know who I am?"

He said, "No, Kevin (our Ops Manager at Best Buy) had some great things to say about you, and I wanted to meet you based on his recommendation."

"Ok, but do you know who my father, Steve Kosnick, is?"

Long audible pause . . .

He said, "Oh, crap!"

The phone call ended there, but my mind did not. I sat back in my chair just two days after being told NO for a raise and made a decision.

I said to myself, "That's what I should be doing!"

The person I had been avoiding, my father, held the keys to the opportunity I had been seeking. This stubborn, young 24-year-old had to eat some humble pie, tuck his tail between his legs, and call his father.

I called him that evening. I am a decisive, Type A personality, after all, so not ceasing the emotional momentum in that moment wasn't in the cards.

He told me, "You can come in for an interview, but you will go through the process and be treated just like anyone else we're considering."

I didn't expect him to say anything different. My father was a very skilled recruiter and leader. Plus, I knew if I did get the opportunity, I'd have a target painted on my back being the boss's eldest son anyhow.

To top it all off, he knew me better than I knew myself at that time in my life. To just hand me an opportunity when I was young and immature, I wouldn't have appreciated it to the degree I should have or made the effort I needed to make it in a business that carries a 7 percent retention rate over five years. Yes, that means that 93 percent of individuals who start as financial advisors don't make it to their fifth year.

As it turned out, I am cut from the same cloth as my father. All the assessments, personality profiling, and interviews showed that I was exactly the type of person with the ability to make it in the financial advisory world.

After going through a number of interviews with others, my father was the last interview. He showed me the financial projections. He also informed me of the downside. This was a 100 percent commission world where if you don't get clients, you don't make a dime.

At the end of the conversation, he extended his hand, beaming with pride, and offered me the opportunity.

> Lesson: When we can get our ego out of the way and lean into humility, doors open.

CHAPTER 2

Chasing Ghosts, Leading Giants

On January 26, 2005, I began my journey as an entrepreneur and started building my financial advisory practice. The life of an advisor, and particularly this company my father represented, wasn't foreign to me whatsoever.

My father started in this career before I was one year old.

I had attended every one of their annual meetings in Milwaukee, WI, since I was a baby. It was like a family reunion to me.

I would love to tell you that my career began with a bang and that it was all sunshine and rainbows, with a straight-line trajectory to success, but that's never how it goes. I was still stuck between two vastly different worlds that I was trying to live simultaneously.

One world was the new entrepreneurial path that I had embarked on.

The other, partying and living a carefree, young adult life.

I found out very quickly that these two worlds cannot coexist successfully. I was burning the candle at both ends, working hard throughout the day and partying four nights a week.

I had a moderately successful first year by most measures. I took on over fifty new clients and earned just over $70,000, which was about 25 percent more than my Best Buy salary.

In year two, I really started to take off. It wasn't because my mind and body were completely run down that I decided to make the change and go all-in on building my business.

No. I'm too stubborn for that.

It was because I heard a rumor.

To this day, I cannot confirm if this rumor was true or not. I confronted the person I heard say it about me, but he has never admitted to it.

I heard that a person I deeply respected and looked up to said that I was "a waste of talent."

That rumor and those words pierced my soul!

It didn't matter if they were actually said or not. The reason that rumor affected me so much was that, in that moment, it was true! I wasn't giving my all to the career or to building a business that could change my life forever.

All my life, I had never been the most talented, fastest, strongest, or smartest, but I would outwork anyone! Most of this was related to sports, but there had also been glimpses in previous work experiences.

An internal switch had been flipped. The gas pedal was pressed to the floor. I was ALL-IN!

I strived to be the first person in the office and the last to leave. I was out to prove this imaginary hater wrong. Turns out, I perform very well with a chip on my shoulder.

I thought if I hit one hundred lives in a year, then I'd belong.

I thought if I hit $100,000, $250,000, $500,000, or $1,000,000 in revenue, then I'd belong.

I thought if I earned designations (letters behind my name), then I'd belong.

I did all of that and then some. None of it worked.

I was chasing ghosts!

> Lesson: There will always be another accomplishment or mountaintop to conquer. Be happy in your progress and the growth you've made.

I kept climbing.

I was building my clientele all week long and studying for tests on the weekends. I had quickly earned my CLU, ChFC, and CLTC designations. I couldn't sit for my CFP because I didn't have a 4-year undergraduate degree.

(A stupid rule by them, in my opinion. I could've had my undergrad in "Underwater Basketweaving" and been able to sit for the exam, but many years in Financial Planning and other designations didn't qualify me per their rules.)

I had passed numerous FINRA exams, including Series 6, 63, 66, 7, 26, 9, and 10.

And I thought I was done with schooling when I dropped out of college.

My self-education had just begun!

On top of all of that, I was soaking in as many self-development and leadership books as I could get my hands on.

In 2007, I was asked to run our intern program. I would advise college students considering a career in financial services. This was my first taste of leadership in the financial services career, as well as recruiting. All of this was on top of continuing to build my financial planning practice.

Essentially two separate full-time jobs packaged as one.

The extra work didn't matter to me because I loved the opportunity to lead like I had been doing prior to starting this career.

I loved every minute of it.

It's a daunting career to figure out at any age, but college students typically had the support of their parents or financial aid, so for many of them, it was the perfect time to try out a commission sales job.

For those who took to it and had some success, they received a full-time offer after graduating and became some of our most successful financial advisors. We had a world-class training and development program for interns. I leaned into it and poured my heart into them. That paid dividends for both our internship program and for me as I continued to progress in my career.

I quickly learned that my passion for leadership was greater than my passion for growing my own practice. I was finding more joy in helping others grow than just growing a book of business.

By that point, I had hired my first team member, and we were working extremely well together.

She handled all the things I was terrible at and that she excelled at, while I focused on seeing existing clients, seeking new clients, and all of my leadership responsibilities.

In 2010, something profound happened; I recruited someone who would change me forever.

I firmly believe that God puts people into our lives for a reason, a season, or a lifetime. It's our job to determine which of those three buckets people fit in. But sometimes, He puts people in our lives that fit all three buckets.

Up until that point, I had recruited, mentored, and developed dozens of new financial advisors. Some left the business quickly, and others are still thriving in that career to this day.

But I always wanted to recruit one that would push me to be my best. One that would compete with me and help bring out that competitive fire that's driven me my entire life. That was a tall order because I was a very good advisor.

Never once did I consider that I would recruit someone who would actually run circles around me.

Perhaps it was naivety, my ego, or my competitiveness. It just never crossed my mind. And no one came close until I met Karl Dettmann.

Karl wasn't our typical recruit. He came from the IT world. He wasn't in sales either, but he did have some history that we looked for.

He was a former collegiate athlete. Not only had he started and run his own business before, but he profiled perfectly. Although he was dyslexic growing up, he overcame that to get through high school, college, and beyond, proving that he could conquer adversity.

It wasn't long before he showed a lot of promise. He was one of the most coachable individuals I had ever encountered.

He kept leaning in and asking questions. He sought counsel not only from me but from anyone who had success in our offices. He was a sponge, but more importantly, he put his head down and did the work required to be successful.

In his first year, he set nationwide company records that stood for seven years before finally being broken in 2017.

He was doing so well that on Sunday evenings, I'd lie in bed and wonder what I was going to say to him in the morning in our Mentor Meeting to challenge him. That forced me to get better as a leader and level up my coaching skills.

Karl didn't just affect me positively; he showed others what was possible. As the old saying goes, "A rising tide lifts all boats." Because Karl was succeeding in such a big way, others sought his advice, learned from him, and wanted to do more for themselves.

> Lesson: Recruit highly talented individuals, and develop them endlessly. Those individuals can lift the entire culture and business to heights never seen before.

By his third full year in the business, he wasn't just competing with me. He was whooping my butt!

Here was the profound moment and a teaching moment for all aspiring leaders out there . . .

When he started to whoop me, I had feelings of joy. I was nothing but proud of him.

Insecure leaders or people would feel envy and jealousy in this scenario. I've seen it firsthand. For me, this was the moment that I knew I was meant to be a leader. I wanted more moments like this where I felt I had a small part in the success of another individual's life.

Not for my own accolades or to claim any credit for their success, but to have that internal feeling of joy, knowing that I either gave them the opportunity to succeed, or my coaching played just a small part in their journey. All credit belongs to Karl in this scenario. He did the work. He was a rockstar financial advisor then and still is to this day.

You know what's better, though?

He's an amazing human being and friend. He and I have experienced the highest of highs and the lowest of lows together.

Karl is in all three buckets for me.

He came into my life for a reason . . . to make me a better leader.

He came into my life for a season . . . while I was his leader at that firm.

And I believe he came into my life for a lifetime, but we're not done yet, so it's too early to tell.

I will be forever grateful to Karl for many things, but perhaps most of all for making me level up and become the best leader I could be.

> Lesson: Never be afraid or too egotistical to recruit the best talent. Recruiting the smartest and most talented people you can find forces you to level up as a leader, and they propel your business to new heights!

CHAPTER 3

Breaking the Curse, Carrying the Torch

From 2013 to 2015, I led the number one district office in the country while also running my own successful financial planning practice.

What made that more impressive was that I was running that office out of Madison, WI. Far from a metropolis, Madison is a mid-size city. We were beating all the big-city offices, including Atlanta, Chicago, Dallas, NYC, LA—you name it.

My time was split nearly 50/50 between the leadership side (mentoring, developing, and recruiting) and the personal practice.

My personal practice team had also grown to three team members. I had a Director of Operations, who handled all paperwork and client services, a Director of Investments, who handled money management, trades, and portfolio design, and a Director of Marketing, who handled my calendar, client outreach, and client events.

These three amazing humans were absolutely instrumental in our success. They allowed me to focus on my crucial tasks and what I was uniquely gifted at.

My calendar was packed, and I loved it!

Tuesday through Thursday, I kept sixteen to twenty client meetings. I dedicated Mondays and Fridays to developing my people and recruiting more of the best talent I could find.

These were some of the most fun years of my career. We had a great young leadership team that loved pouring into others to get new advisors off to a fast start in their careers. Our retention rate of new advisors was nearly 30 percent (the industry average was 7 percent at that time).

Because of our success, I was beginning to be looked at and assessed to be one of the next Managing Partners within the company. At the time, the company had an incredible Leadership Development Program that I was privileged to be a part of, and I was on the fast track just eight short years into my career to the highest level of leadership.

There was a problem, though.

Although it seemed certain that I would become a Managing Partner, I wasn't certain that I wanted the role.

Beyond the fact that I absolutely loved what I was doing, that was my Father's role as owner of our firm. My teenage years were spent watching him, utterly stressed out and taking that out on me. (Side note: I was not an easy teenager and deserved a big portion of his wrath.)

In 1993, my Father took over that firm. At the time, it was ranked 103 out of 105 firms across the country. Since then, there's been considerable consolidation down to seventy-five firms, and during his tenure, he took the firm from that lowly position to a top-quartile firm in a small market.

I was in eighth grade when we moved to Madison, WI, from Central Illinois. It was a tough time to move at thirteen years old, leaving all my friends and being the new kid while having to make new friends.

Not to mention, we were Chicago Bears fans moving to the enemy territory of Packerland. That in and of itself has created some mental resiliency over the years.

Moving at any point in your life can be difficult, but it's particularly difficult in your teenage years. As I was trying to navigate my new world, my Father was trying to build a firm with the stress of the world on his shoulders. This dynamic led to us butting heads a lot, starting in middle school and into my early twenties.

He wasn't just the owner of the firm—the firm was so unequipped to grow at the time—he was the recruiter, the trainer, the sales expert, everything.

When you combine the stress he was under and my teenage rebellious spirit, let's just say, we didn't mesh well. Many nights would end with us yelling at each other. I knew exactly how to push his buttons because I was just like him in many ways.

I remember one evening in particular, I was sitting at the kitchen table working on some homework that I undoubtedly waited to the last minute to finish. We were getting into it. For the life of me, I cannot remember what it was about, but we were both hot.

I continued sitting at the three-inch thick, solid oak kitchen table while speaking my piece as he would yell back from the family room, no more than ten feet away. My mother was calmly doing dishes as she was rendered helpless when the two of us were at each other's throats.

I hit the inferno button inside of him.

I said, "How am I supposed to act how you want me to act when all you do is piss me off?"

That got him out of his chair real quick.

In a split second, he was hovering over me, all six feet three inches of him as he said, "I piss you off?"

Boom!

His hammer fist came down on the solid oak table. Instead of hitting his oldest son (which, to be very clear, he never did), he hit the table as hard as he could.

The yelling immediately stopped. He went back to his chair in the family room, and it was quiet . . . for a moment.

Then, loud and erratic snoring.

My mom and I both went out to my father, where we found him passed out in his chair.

He must've known something was wrong, which was why he went back to his chair immediately following punching that table. The pain caused him to pass out. He hit that solid oak table so hard that he suffered a boxer's fracture in his right hand.

I don't remember either of us ever apologizing to each other.

Feelings weren't really ever communicated between us at that juncture in our lives. Those were reserved for us kids and our Mother. She was our emotional support growing up. She is one of the kindest, most loving humans on the planet and has never met a stranger.

My dad grew up not hearing words of affirmation or I love you's. His dad, my grandfather Howard, worked two jobs to support his family after he got out of the Navy.

When my dad became a teenager, he began to work. His family was so poor at one point that they couldn't afford to buy him a baseball glove to play baseball or even catch with his friends.

He worked hard in his teenage years and was able to buy a boat as they lived on the Illinois River, and he loved to water ski. Then, he bought a sweet muscle car, a bronze colored 1968 Charger.

He raised us boys like he was raised.

I can count on one hand how many times I heard the words "I love you" from him growing up. No matter how good I was at sports, and sports were definitely my strength over school, I couldn't get the words of affirmation I so desperately craved from him. In hindsight, that's most certainly what drove my rebellious spirit in my teenage years and why I fought back with him so much.

The reason I'm telling you all of this is that it directly correlates with my apprehension about becoming a Managing Partner.

I wasn't sure I wanted the role because I saw how it affected my father when I was growing up, and I didn't want it to affect me and subsequently my relationships with my kids.

While those unsettled feelings were going on inside of me, I kept working hard and striving to be better as both an advisor and a leader. I continued on in the company's Leadership Development Program. Meanwhile, I was still on their short list for candidates to become a Managing Partner.

At one of our Leadership Development Program meetups, I spoke those unsettled feelings out loud to a couple of friends. One of them decided to be candid with me that day, and I'm so grateful that he did. We were doing a Visioning exercise whose goal was to write a Vision so compelling that it could be a keynote speech.

I was getting great feedback on my Vision and my talk. I am a Visionary, so that part of the exercise comes pretty naturally to me.

Then, my friend spoke these words over me: "Josh, I keep hearing you say that you don't want to become a Managing Partner, but every step or move you make says otherwise."

> Lesson: Always have truth tellers in your life! These individuals are your real friends. They call you out on your BS, and they tell you what you need to hear, not just what you want to hear.

He was right!

I needed to hear those words.

We then got the opportunity to have a beautiful conversation about the role. I gained perspective and permission to be a Managing Partner AND the husband and father I wanted to be.

You see, it wasn't the role in and of itself that I had a problem with. It was how my father handled the role and our relationship at the time. Although I am my father's son, that doesn't mean I have to operate at the office or in my home the way that he did.

I get to choose the leader and the man I want to be.

The timing of this conversation couldn't have been more perfect, as my father had recently notified corporate of his retirement date, October 31, 2016. I had two years to get my house in order and prove I was the best man for the job.

It was like God was speaking right through this friend and delivering the exact words I needed to hear.

> Lesson: We were all raised a certain way. I truly believe that most parents do their best to raise their kids and give them the best opportunities in life. That being said, when we become adults and choose to have our own families, we are left with a choice. Will I raise my kids the way I was raised? Is there a generational curse that I'm going to break?

For my father, he chose to break the generational curse of money in our family. No longer would the Kosnicks reside in the lower class. I'm so happy and blessed he made that choice for us. All of his hard work allowed us kids to never be in need or left out with our friends.

If we wanted to play baseball, he could afford to buy us a glove. Even though it was never said, I can only imagine how proud he was of himself and us while watching us play baseball and every other sport, knowing that he wasn't able to as a kid. He changed our family tree forever, and all of his sons have gone on to lead highly successful lives with amazing families.

For me, I chose to break the generational curse of not expressing our feelings. I tell my kids that I love them every single day, and most days, more than once. I tell them that I'm proud of them as often as I can, but more importantly, I make sure that they're proud of themselves.

CHAPTER 4

Strive to Never Arrive

On May 26, 2016, I got the call.

I was on the golf course. It was a picture-perfect morning. The sun was shining down on us, and we were playing a beautiful course called Wild Rock in Wisconsin Dells. The deer are so protected and unafraid there that they'll walk up to you on the tee box.

Every year, we would take some of our top advisors on a mini-trip to the Dells for some golf, a great dinner, and a world-class spa called Sundara the next morning. I have some cherished memories from those trips.

Two months prior to that morning, I was in Milwaukee, WI, interviewing for the big job. At just thirty-five years old and only eleven years into my career, I was interviewing to succeed my father as Managing Partner. Although he wanted the job to be mine, it wasn't his decision. The leadership team of the Fortune 80 company we represented made those decisions and appointments.

There was some contention and uncertainty about my being chosen, even though my resume was one of the top in the country. There had been some previous examples of sons succeeding their fathers within the company that hadn't gone so well. Not only that, the optics of nepotism were lingering, even though putting my resume up against anyone else's should've quelled any doubters.

Nonetheless, I put my best foot forward that day and prayed for the best outcome. My wife and I really loved

Madison and didn't want to move to another city if they chose someone else and offered me another opportunity.

When I got the call, butterflies circled my stomach. I told the rest of my foursome to continue on, promising to catch up to them when I was off the phone.

"Josh, your plan for growth for Southern Wisconsin and Northern Illinois was well-received here by all of the leadership team. We wanted to let you know that we've chosen you to be our next Managing Partner in Madison, WI."

The phone call was about twenty-five minutes long, but those words are the only ones I can remember from that call.

I called my wife, Jenna, with tears in my eyes right after I hung up with the corporate leaders.

"Hey, babe, how would you like to stay in Madison for the foreseeable future?"

It was such a joyous moment for both of us.

We had been through so many years of hard work, with her supporting me every step of the way. She would support me no matter what, but she really didn't want to have to move further away from her family either. We had three little girls at that time, and she was handling everything with such grace and class.

At the end of the eighteen holes, we proceeded to the clubhouse before we headed back out for our scramble round. My father was waiting for me. He had the biggest smile on his face.

I'm not sure if the corporate leaders called him before or after they called me, but he knew. He gave me the biggest hug, and he told me how proud he was of me. Those words I so desperately wanted from him as a kid, I got now, along with a warm embrace.

Working with my father for eleven years wasn't always a smooth road. Ask any family-owned business, and you'll find there is dysfunction at some level or another when working with family members. It comes with the territory.

That being said, those eleven years were the best years of our relationship. Everything I wanted from my dad as a kid, I got as an adult while working with him.

All the love, the praise, and the affirmations came during that time period.

I got to see my father at his best. He wasn't just a tremendous leader and business owner, but I also got to experience the best dad he could be while working under his leadership.

I will be forever grateful for that time together and all the ways he helped me grow as a leader and a man.

October 26, 2016, was a special night. Not only were my Chicago Cubs in the World Series for the first time in 108 years, but we also had a passing of the torch event.

Family, friends, colleagues, and team members came to Madison to celebrate my dad's retirement and my installation as the next Managing Partner. It was a wonderful dinner, party, and celebration for both of us.

We both got to speak from our hearts to the crowd, and that evening, we got to celebrate each other.

We honored my dad for the incredible legacy he was leaving behind and sent both my parents off into a well-earned retirement.

And for me . . . the next chapter was just beginning.

My official contract date was November 1, 2016.

That's when I became THE leader of the firm.

There's an odd thing that happens when you transition from A leader in the company to THE leader of the company. Every single relationship you have within the organization changes overnight.

People start looking at you and treating you differently. And it's not always a good thing. In fact, it's mostly fake and weird. I never changed who I was, and I didn't anticipate anyone else changing who they were just because my title or position changed, but they did.

As A leader, you're seen as one of them. You can hang out, you can commiserate, and just be. As THE leader, that all goes away. They position themselves around you to see what you can do for them, or they pick their spots to hang out with you because having a relationship with you may benefit them in the future.

This was a hard but good lesson to learn early on.

As the leader of a company, it's up to you to set the tone, create the culture, and drive the team toward a common vision. Having friendships needs to take a backseat to the above. When you're the leader, it's far greater to be respected than to be liked. In short, you have to be the adult in the room at all times.

I have been so blessed to have tremendous mentors and coaches in my life. My father and John Wright Sr. were two who were absolutely indispensable. They both gave me a similar message as I took over.

As Managing Partner, you have four key roles. If you do them effectively, you will have a magnificent career and build an incredible business.

Those four key roles are:

1. Recruit the best talent.
2. Develop that talent endlessly.
3. Run and maintain strong finances.
4. Build and keep a great culture.

> Lesson: This isn't just great advice for the Managing Partner of a financial firm. This is excellent advice for both entrepreneurs and business owners.

When individuals have role clarity, it's incredible what they can do. That is as true for the leader as it is for a frontline employee. I had role clarity and a hunger to build upon the legacy my father had begun within the firm. I didn't just want to maintain the success he left me but take the firm to new heights.

I learned along the way that having a motto or rallying cry for the year can be very powerful. My first motto after taking over the firm was "Strive to never arrive."

It was as much for me as for everyone I led. It was a nod to a statement my father drilled into my head growing up: "We're either green and growing, or we're ripe and rotting."

In other words, there is no staying the same.

I had seen plenty of other Managing Partners significantly increase their lifestyle the moment they took over their firms or even let off the gas like they had "made it." I didn't want to do either of those things.

My motivation was to be the very best I could be so that the firm and everyone in it could be the very best they could be. Striving to never arrive carried us through year one, as we had some ambitious goals to achieve.

We recruited well. I had one of the very best recruiters in the country. I had brought him into the firm years before, and our relationship continued to grow. As I poured myself into him, he continued to be loyal and extremely productive. He was an incredible asset.

As a leadership team, we were recruiting between forty to fifty advisors per year. Our development culture was strong and only getting better.

Our internship program was also a strength. We recruited around sixty college interns each year. They were a pipeline for us and produced some of our very best full-time financial advisors. We could mold them without the baggage or bad habits that can carry over from other careers that have a stable salary.

In short, we were having fun.

We had our share of issues, but we felt like we could overcome all of them as a leadership team. We were being recognized nationally for our recruiting, internships, and development.

Then, 2020 happened.

Our motto entering this year was, "Hold Fast, Stay True." A nod to the old Navy, and boy, it was the perfect motto heading into a turbulent year.

On March 11, 2020, I was in Cedar Rapids, IA, celebrating my great friend Kalvin Grabau-Keele as he was just appointed Managing Partner. It was a wonderful evening with friends, but dark clouds were looming.

In that ballroom of about 200 people, we were there with some corporate leaders, who were discussing what was to come with this new pandemic called COVID-19. The company had to make plans, prepare, and provide guidance for offices in all fifty states.

The very next day, the same leaders who were with me in Cedar Rapids, IA, called to let me know that I should cancel my recognition dinner for our top advisors, scheduled for that Friday evening.

The next couple of weeks were a blur, but the state of Wisconsin set out its rules and guidelines for us to follow.

I had to inform about 250 advisors, team members, and employees that we were closing our offices, and they would work from home for a couple of weeks. I was extremely unsettled by this, not because it could have significant financial ramifications but because none of the rules and guidelines made sense to me.

Nonetheless, I let the pressure from corporate guide my decision to close my offices for a period, despite my best judgment.

I did have anxiety over this, but I couldn't let that show. As the leader, it's my job to remain calm under duress. It's to be that lighthouse that our people can count on, the calm in the storm.

In our profession, we have always operated face-to-face with our clients. Our trust was built on that human connection. We are dealing with people's hard-earned money. We sat in our offices and their homes at the kitchen table with them.

Sending 250 people to work from home and work entirely on Zoom was certainly unprecedented. Even though digital tools like Skype had been around for about a decade, working through that technology was very uncommon at the time.

We got everyone the technology they needed to work from home, and things were going as well as they could. Our corporate office in Milwaukee did a great job of working quickly to help us adapt.

What they couldn't do, and what became the hardest part of individuals working from home, was managing their emotions.

As I was working from home at that time, I had four young kids running around, stomping like elephants on the floor above me as I sat in my home office. My day would start around 7 a.m., and most days wouldn't end until 9 p.m. My meetings were typically done by 4 or 5 p.m., but then the calls came.

Every single night, I was talking to a leader, team member, or employee off the edge. I became a psychologist overnight. During the day, I operated mostly as a normal business owner and firm leader. By night, I became the in-house psychiatrist.

As humans, we are built for connection. We are built for community and relationships. When we were separated and isolated in our own homes, we lost all of the community that we relied on.

Gone were the high-fives. Gone were the hugs. Gone were the food and drinks with friends, where we could bond together.

When inmates do something wrong in prison, they are sent to solitary confinement for a duration of time. Prison, in and of itself, is seen as one of the harshest punishments in our modern society. Yet, when the worst of the worst do something wrong in prison, they're sent to solitary confinement, otherwise known as "the hole."

Why would authorities utilize solitary confinement to punish their prisoners?

Because it's much, much worse!

In fact, there are many advocacy groups pressuring politicians to end solitary confinement due to the psychological damage it can cause. Even the United Nations has written "The Mandela Rules," which classifies solitary confinement lasting more than 15 days as a form of **torture** due to its detrimental effects on mental health.

I witnessed the psychological toll firsthand while we were confined to our homes during COVID-19 in 2020. Some of my best advisors and staff were having a hard time, including one of my key leaders. This one caught me off guard because of all people, I thought I'd need to worry about her least. She was an introvert by nature and just a tremendous worker and asset to the firm.

It turns out that there's a major difference between being introverted by choice and being forced to be introverted due to a lockdown. She was handling a lot at the time, putting in a lot of work to keep the team's spirits up as well. It was my responsibility to support her and keep her spirits high enough to continue leading.

As soon as the lockdown lifted, I got us back in the office. That didn't come without controversy, but I knew we needed each other. We were fortunate that everyone had a separate workstation and office in our main office, which was about 35,000 square feet.

We allowed people to come back as they were comfortable. If someone felt more comfortable wearing a mask, they could wear one. If they didn't want to wear one, they didn't have to.

My one rule was that we wouldn't shame each other for our choices. We would support each other during this divisive time in our history, and, most of all, we would do what we do best: serve our clients.

We found a new way to work through the tumultuous year.

We embraced Zoom technology, and so did our clients. It turned out to be a blessing in disguise. It wasn't as hard as we anticipated to build trust through computer screens.

Prior to 2020, 90 percent of our client meetings were face-to-face. In 2020, that ratio flipped, and 90 percent of our client meetings were virtual. This new world allowed us to be more efficient. We didn't have to drive to as many meetings, and our clients didn't have to drive to us.

By the end of 2020, we had a record year in almost every revenue category, and we were up 30 percent in the category we tracked most. As we weathered the worst of the storm as a team, we were poised to have an epic year in 2021.

CHAPTER 5

The Fall

January 2021 started like any other year.

We had so much momentum behind us after weathering the worst of the pandemic storm, and we had BIG goals set to be conquered.

It wasn't too far into the year before a major storm brewed.

In February, my compliance officer intercepted an ominous email from one of my young leaders. We'll call him Richard for the remainder of this story. Before I tell you what was in that email, it is important to go back and tell you how we got here.

In early 2017, I was visiting with a group of my friends. These were my guys. I played football with most of them.

That day, I was introduced to one of my friend's sons, Richard. He was fresh out of college, engaged to be married, expecting his first child, and eager to make a living to support his young family. Not long after that introduction, I offered Richard an opportunity to join our firm and become a financial advisor.

Richard got off to a decent start. Likeable and charismatic, he was extremely eager to learn and grow. The more effort he put in, the more I grew a fondness for him and wanted to help.

At that time, he was a similar size to me, and I gave him thousands of dollars' worth of custom suits from my own closet as a reward because I knew it would help level up his confidence. "Look good, feel good, do good" was a mantra at the time.

I mentored Richard weekly, sharing as much knowledge as I could to help him succeed in this challenging industry, and our friendship continued to grow over the years.

He was young and immature, but I had developed plenty of young men and women before through similar immaturities. His talent was in attracting individuals into our business, and recruiting talent was one of our top priorities.

The problem was that he wasn't good at developing that talent, leading to the individuals leaving just as quickly as they arrived. It is very expensive for a business owner to constantly recruit new talent, develop them, and get them up and running.

About eighteen months before that ominous email, Richard called a meeting with me and my corporate liaison, where he delivered an ultimatum:

"Make me a Managing Director, or I'm leaving."

He went on to tell me that he had an offer from a competing firm for $500,000 to take on that role. The problem for him was that I had a relationship with the Managing Partner at that firm, and I called him on his bluff. That offer never existed.

It's important to note that I was developing him towards that end, but he wasn't ready yet. His compliance record fell below our standards, he had numerous complaints for verbal harassment by female staff members, he attempted to run illegal sales contests (that we caught before damage could be done, and he hadn't passed a required FINRA exam to be named to that position)—the list goes on.

In that moment, I had a very difficult decision to make, one I knew I shouldn't make alone. I called in the rest of my executive leadership team to let them know exactly what happened and make a decision about Richard's future with the firm.

Whatever the decision would end up being, it was important to me that my leadership team played a role in it because it would shape the future of the firm.

> Lesson: When people are part of the plan, they don't fight the plan.

The difficult choice before us was this:

- Fire Richard and potentially compete against him in the marketplace
- Work with Richard to become a better leader and team player

To add to the decision's complexity, I knew if we chose to fire him, he would sue us for discrimination. Not because he was actually discriminated against but because of his vindictive nature.

My leadership team, my corporate liaison, and I had a very deep discussion exploring all possibilities and what the potential outcomes might be. In the end, we chose to work with Richard, to lean in and help him become the best version of the talented individual we all saw.

Things began to slowly get better—or so I thought.

I also hired a consultant to work with Richard. A great leader who had just come back to Madison. He had a tremendous resume in banking and in our industry, developing advisors and leaders. The other key attribute he had working in his favor that I didn't is that he is also black.

I had never in my life made skin color an issue. I've always made it a point to treat people with dignity and respect. I actually believe that anyone who bases issues on race operates with the lowest form of intelligence in the human race.

But for Richard, everything was about race, so I brought in this consultant and paid him very well so that Richard would have a confidant as well as another leader to pour into his life.

I was continuing to meet with Richard weekly, working on his leadership and development skills, along with improving his knowledge of compliance and doing things the right way. Unbeknownst to me, Richard was secretly recording our conversations and plotting the entire time.

Back to the "ominous email" we intercepted.

This email that Richard sent to corporate included a PowerPoint with some links to recordings that were clearly spliced together. Anyone who's ever listened to anything could tell that, but what for?

The PowerPoint would explain that.

Richard detailed incidents, lies, and embellishments to paint me and our carefully built great culture as racist and toxic. At the end was another ultimatum, this time for the corporate office.

Richard wanted his own office and was willing to do whatever it took to see that happen. I wasn't willing to invest in one for him at that time for the reasons above.

The investment would've been somewhere between $250,000 and $500,000. I would've had no problem with that investment for the right person with the right motivations. Richard's motivation was centered around being out from underneath my team's supervision.

He didn't realize that compliance was our strength, that we not only had to comply with FINRA and SEC laws but also our own company standards.

Following these laws and standards keeps clients' best interests at heart. Following these laws and standards keeps your name out of the paper and ensures you don't become the next Bernie Madoff.

It turns out that when you box someone with narcissistic tendencies into a corner, it's like boxing a tiger into a corner. They become vicious as a mode of survival!

In hindsight, I can see now that my coaching him to improve in these areas wasn't taken that way by Richard. He took it as a restraint on his freedom or a threat to his survival. With those feelings, he did what he did because he thought that's what survival was.

> Lesson: Narcissists are cancerous in an organization. Rid them from your culture before they metastasize and take down your whole organization.

I had a meeting with my corporate liaison discussing the contents of this ominous email. Because that liaison was so involved with our firm over the past couple of years, he knew that the contents of that email were largely BS.

Either way, I had another very difficult decision to make.

There were no more second chances this time. The relationship between Richard and me was fractured, to say the least.

My liaison asked me what I was going to do.

I said, "If I fire him, I'm certainly getting sued. It's also a firm 'no' that he sets up shop under the same umbrella in my territory. What if I release him like a free agent, and he can interview other Managing Partners throughout the country to see if they're a better fit for him?"

That was our decision.

Richard interviewed with a dozen different firms within our system and received one offer from one of my Managing Partner friends. Even though Richard betrayed me at a very high level, I still wanted what was best for him.

When that friend called me to inquire about Richard, I told him the truth and also made sure to highlight Richard's talents. Perhaps, a different leader would be a breath of fresh air for him. That was the hope for all parties involved.

And just like that, Richard moved, which meant my leadership team and I could get back to our goals for 2021. There was a breath of fresh air for us as well. Richard's poisonous attitude had been removed.

When you remove a cancer from the culture, the rest of the team has a pretty visceral reaction. Whether it's stated out loud or just with their eyes, they say, "What took you so long?"

> Lesson: Most of us have heard the expression "hire slow, fire fast." I believe that statement is incomplete. In the middle of those two should be "lean in" because it is expensive to replace people. That being said, if you've done the "leaning in" to develop them and they still don't respond, it's time to let go as quickly as possible. They've overstayed their welcome.

CHAPTER 6

A Knock at the Door

In April of 2021, I was at home playing with my kids in our family room when there was a knock at our front door.

I answered to find a plain-looking dude who could've been out doing a survey or trying to get me to invest in solar. Instead, he handed me an envelope and carefully stated, "You've been served."

The lawsuit I had feared would come was now at my doorstep ... literally!

It's one thing to be called names, it's another for someone to lie about your name, but for someone you cared about and did everything to help, to put your name in legal documents accusing you of heinous activity is a feeling I don't wish on anyone.

Reading through the accusations wasn't too surprising. Much of what was in those documents was in that ominous email to corporate. Richard had placed my name in stories that I wasn't even a part of. He told stories in legal form that didn't even happen.

Richard had hired an ambulance-chasing attorney. You know the type, they have billboards all over the highways and only get paid if they win or there's a settlement.

The next day, I forwarded the papers to corporate for their guidance and assistance. They had a robust legal team and had dealt with far worse than this over the years, so I knew they would know what to do.

They advised me to hire my own attorney and start getting my ducks in a row, stating they would help me as much as they could. Though I was too naïve to know it at the time, they were placating me.

When I was in college, one of my hobbies was riding motorcycles. Crotch rockets to be exact. In that community, if you've ridden long enough, you know it's not a matter of "if" you put one down, but "when." I was fortunate enough to give up that hobby before I was in a major accident.

The same is true in life as a business owner. It's not a matter of "if" you get sued, but rather "when."

I suppose this being my third business, I should've felt fortunate that it was my very first lawsuit, but I did not. The lawsuit and the lies being said about me were unsettling, to put it mildly.

As the leader of the firm, I couldn't let my emotions impact how I led; we still had a job to do. For the time being, I decided to bury those emotions as much as I could and keep focused on the job at hand. I continued to lead and pour into my people.

June 16, 2021

What started as a perfectly normal morning turned into my world becoming completely undone.

I woke up at 5:04 a.m. like any normal day. I had a regimented morning routine that consisted of hydration, exercise, Wim Hof breathing exercises, prayer, and reading.

By the time I was out of the shower, my cell phone rang.

It was a corporate Executive VP that I was expecting later that morning at my office. It was time for us to renegotiate our recruiting and production targets.

The phone call wasn't unexpected, but the result was . . . "Josh, we got into town a bit early today. Can you meet us at the Marriott?"

I said, sure. I'm almost ready.

Have you ever gotten one of those sinking feelings in your gut, like something really bad is about to happen? Ya, my stomach was on the floor as I hung up that call.

The entire eight-minute drive from my home to the Marriott, my head was tossing back and forth, thinking about the possibilities of what I was about to walk into.

My office was only one-tenth of a mile away from that Marriott. Why would we be meeting there if it wasn't something bad? But the office is crushing it right now and putting up numbers never seen before. Why would they get rid of me and jeopardize that?

I walked confidently to them with my iPad in hand in case I needed to take notes. I shook their hands, and as soon as my butt hit the chair, the Executive VP said to me, "Josh, there's no easy way to say this, we're moving in a different direction, and you are no longer Managing Partner."

As my brain tried to process what was just said to me, time slowed down.

I looked around the lobby and noticed a couple of familiar faces, security detail for corporate executives I've known for several years. They were there for protection in case I became a problem.

It was like being in a movie for a brief moment.

As I came back to reality, the Executive VP showed me two pieces of paper with minimal words on them and asked me to sign one of them. I had just enough wits about me not to sign anything at that moment.

I said, "I've trusted you guys my entire career, but today, I'm not signing anything until I speak with my attorney."

I don't think I was in that Marriott for more than a few minutes. I walked out and got in my car to begin my eight-minute drive home. I didn't make it too far down the road before I had to stop and pull off into a parking lot. I couldn't see.

I couldn't see because I was bawling.

I sat in that parking lot for about half an hour trying to gather my thoughts and gain my composure.

"What am I going to tell my family?"

"What can I even say to my dad? The man who built this firm from the ground up and left a legacy for me."

"How did this go so very wrong?"

"Why would they say that they would help me and instead terminate me?"

I tried to check my calendar and email to see if I needed to take care of anything, but my access was shut down the moment I walked out of the Marriott.

I often wonder if anyone saw me that morning. All alone in my car, crying. There were plenty of people around, unloading their bikes to go on the Capital City Trail as it was shaping up to be a beautiful day. No one stopped by to see if I was okay, though. Perhaps they didn't see me, or maybe they were too uncomfortable with the sight of a man in such desperation.

(There's something odd about our society that when we see a man cry, we immediately think it's a sign of weakness. We don't have the empathy we do for women or children in the same situation. And this notion is killing our men.)

I finally gathered myself enough to make the rest of the short trek home. As I pulled into the garage, my wife, Jenna, met me at the door. It was extremely odd for me to be home by 9 a.m., so she must've sensed something was wrong.

I could barely look her in the eyes as I stated, "I'm done."

She hugged me and asked, "What are we going to do?"

I said, "It's not the time for that question."

I got my expensive suit off and made my way to my basement, where I lay in our spare bedroom in the fetal position, crying. Jenna lay with me for hours.

After I walked out of the Marriott that morning, the corporate executives ran their playbook. They called an emergency virtual Town Hall across all the offices that I still held leases on. In that virtual Town Hall, they announced my termination and, in the very next breath, introduced my successor.

My phone was blowing up all morning with texts, calls, and voicemails from my team expressing anger, frustration, and sympathy.

Although I appreciated the love from them, it tore my heart open more every time my phone buzzed. The texts and voice mails ranged from them expressing how much my leadership has meant to them and that they wouldn't be where they are today without me, to figuring out a way to stage a coup and leave the company altogether.

> Journal Entry: "I cry daily now. That's a new development in my life. I've never been much of a 'crier' before this. Sometimes, it's because of a text that comes in, and their words get to me. Sometimes, it's because something triggered a memory. I miss my people. I miss leading them. I miss pouring my life into theirs and helping them develop into more awesome versions of themselves. It brought me so much joy."

I found out that advisors were emailing the CEO of the company, expressing their feelings and letting them know how bad a mistake they had made. Nothing changed, though. I was done, and they weren't going to change their minds after naming a successor that quickly.

One of the hardest conversations I had was with my youngest brother, Jordan. He was one of the leaders within the firm on my executive leadership team. He undoubtedly had my back; he always has, but he wanted to know what to do with himself after what just happened to me. His love and support have always meant the world to me.

My advice: "Keep doing your job. You have a family to feed. I'll be in touch with you as I figure things out."

The corporate leaders told him to take a couple of weeks off. They were either trying to remove his influence from the office, fearing he'd act out or be too emotional to lead after what happened to his older brother.

Either way, the advice they gave him was completely tone deaf. His job as an advisor was 100 percent commission and advisory fees. He didn't have paid time off like normal W-2 employees. On top of that, he had clients to serve.

One of the hardest things for me to grapple with that day was that I couldn't be there to comfort and protect my people. They were experiencing a range of emotions, including anger, sadness, grief, uncertainty, and fear. "If they could do this to their leader, they could do this to anyone" was a comment I later heard expressed that day. The texts and calls kept coming for weeks, and every time, I'd break down again.

Amongst all of the noise in my head during this time, I heard a whisper. A whisper that can only be described as God's voice: "You're free."

At the time, I did NOT want to hear it. I didn't want to be free. I was enjoying what I was doing. My plan was to run that company from ages 36 through 56, grow it as big as possible, and then figure out what my second act would be.

Well, as the old adage goes, "If you want to make God laugh, tell Him your plans."

I felt completely betrayed. Now, in the midst of two legal battles, I was all alone. I was stabbed in the back by Richard, whom I brought into the business and mentored to success.

Now, the second knife came in from the company that I had grown up in and admired my entire life.

CHAPTER 7

The Power of the Pause

I made an important decision fairly quickly in the days following my termination. I chose to avoid quick decisions; I didn't want to make an emotional decision that I might regret later.

I knew I'd be a hot commodity in the financial services world. My phone was already ringing with competitors trying to lure me in. But my mind and emotions weren't there yet.

Rather than being driven by spite or vengeance, I wanted to make a decision about my future that was rooted in love and what was best for my family and me moving forward.

So, I decided to take the summer off. When else would I ever be able to spend an entire summer with my kids while they're growing up? We had an amazing time together and created some lifelong memories. Also, I've never played more golf than I did.

But something more important was happening.

I was in a dark spot mentally and emotionally. As much as I was physically present with my family, my mind was often elsewhere.

I spent many evenings out by my fire pit in the backyard, overlooking the golf course with a bourbon and a cigar in hand. I spent those evenings in conversation with God.

"Why did this happen to me?"

"Wasn't I serving my purpose in life?"

"How do I move forward from here?"

"You must have a heckuva plan in place for me to be going through this pain."

I want to make an important distinction here, though. I wasn't drinking my sorrows away. I rarely had more than one pour of bourbon. Rather, I was leaning in and processing all of my emotions. I was going through the stages of grief. All the feelings I had, from anger and betrayal to sadness and sorrow, were being processed internally.

I felt every bit of pain. I wanted to. I didn't want this inflection point in my life to slip by without it becoming an inspection point.

> Lesson: Never let the inflection points in your life pass you by without deep inspection and reflection!

We've always asked and taught our kids since the moment they could walk, "What do we do when we fall down? We get back up." What kind of example would I be for my kids if I didn't pick myself back up after getting kicked down? It doesn't matter how hard the fall is; we must rise again, brush ourselves off, and keep moving forward.

One of the hardest realizations I had was that my identity was wrapped up in my career and my title. I had worked so hard to get to that mountain top, and I still saw so much growth to go.

When that was ripped away from me, there was suddenly a question I couldn't answer: "Who am I?"

When our career or job title is how we identify in life, a sudden loss or change can drive deep depression and a lack of self.

I was soul-searching.

Through that soul-searching, I came to realize that I am not *what* I do. None of us is. That is just a part of who we are.

I am a child of God.
I am a loving son.
I am an older brother.
I am a husband.
I am a father.
I am a caring friend.
I am an athlete.
I am a leader.
I am a visionary.

I could go on with my list, but you get the idea.

As humans, we are a giant puzzle. All puzzles are comprised of smaller pieces that fit together.

Who we are is a collection of smaller pieces that form the physical form that stands before others each and every day.

Who are you?

I encourage you to begin making your list, knowing that you are far more than your job or title.

The summer passed quickly, and we sent our kids back to school that fall.

There was still no end in sight with my negotiations with corporate on my exit. When lawyers are involved, everything takes longer. With the kids out of the house during the day, I had a lot more time to myself. My mind was still fragile, and now, I was getting antsy on top of it.

I'm a driven, Type-A individual who likes to be working towards a vision. Not working, not serving a purpose in this world, was completely foreign to me, and it was taking even more of a toll on my psyche.

I started taking interviews and having conversations with other firms and people in the industry. Something profoundly odd was happening after those interviews and conversations, though.

I had spent the last seventeen years in this industry, so the meetings should've been just business as usual. Instead, I left each meeting feeling more unsettled. Each time I left a conversation or meeting, I had this weird feeling in my gut. It took a lot of prayer and reflection to determine why that feeling was happening.

The easiest thing for me would've been to sign with a competing company and do what I was doing, or to start my own firm and build it up again. The vast majority of my advisors and staff would've joined me. Not only did my former corporate office know that, but it was what they feared most.

What God was telling me in those moments of reflection was that I had already accomplished everything I set out to accomplish in that industry. It was time to blaze a new trail.

As easy as it is for me to state that now, it was a mighty tough pill to swallow in the moment. Not to mention, if that were true, what would I do next?

I was working with my coach at the time every other week. I must give my friend and coach, Jason Teteak, a mountain of credit for keeping my head screwed on straight throughout this dark period. I tried to push him away after my termination. My thought was, you're my business coach, and I no longer have a business for us to talk about.

He had a very wise response: "Josh, I have a feeling you're going to need me more now than ever."

He was so right!

Together, we constructed a really simple yet profound tool.

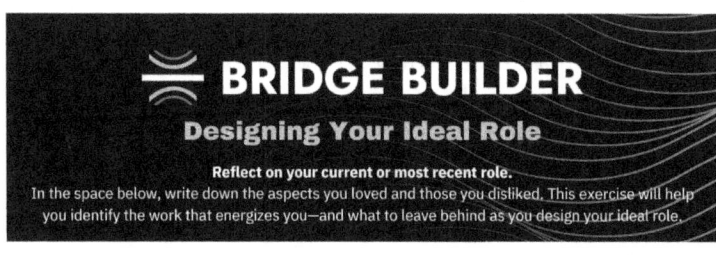

This image is protected via Instant IP^{IP}.

We created our own version of a T-chart. For any of you financial gurus out there who normally see assets and liabilities labeled on a T-chart, this was something very different.

We drew a line down the middle of the paper.

At the top left, we wrote, "What did you love about your previous role?"

At the top right, we wrote, "What did you dislike about your previous role?"

I began my lists.

Under things I loved were things like . . .

- ✓ Training and developing people
- ✓ Mentoring
- ✓ Helping others see visions for themselves and making them come to reality
- ✓ Working towards BIG goals with a team
- ✓ Visioning a bigger and brighter future for the organization
- ✓ Recruiting and helping others build their teams
- ✓ Solving big issues

Under things I disliked . . .

- ✗ Dealing with restraints from compliance
- ✗ FINRA
- ✗ SEC
- ✗ Dealing with the politics of corporate executives
- ✗ Problems caused by others, in particular narcissistic advisors

Then I asked myself a very important question: What if I could design a world where I only did the things I loved to do and mitigated or eliminated everything I disliked?

I was onto something but still had zero clue how I was going to do it. I was now receiving offers from competing firms ... BIG offers. To put into perspective how big a decision I was facing, I had a multi-million-dollar offer from a company to do almost exactly what I was doing before.

I have a family to support, and I'm very competitive. It certainly would've been the easy thing for me to accept that offer and continue doing what I've been doing for seventeen years. Though I was wrestling with a desire for revenge, I didn't want it to be a driving factor in my decision.

Vengeance is darkside energy, and although it is powerful, it can lead you to do some things outside of your character. I felt that if I let that vengeance consume me, along with my competitive spirit, I might hurt someone I care about in the process.

I decided to push that company off as I continued to heal and gain more clarity on my future.

Disrespect will close doors that apologies can't reopen.

—Unknown

CHAPTER 8

They're Watching

I had never been into journaling or had a diary growing up. I wasn't a great English student and hated writing papers. (I get the irony here as I'm writing this book.)

That being said, I have never been against journaling. I didn't think it was dumb; I just never took the time to do it.

In fact, many of my friends and mentors had spoken very highly of the practice. It was Jason, my coach, who encouraged me to journal throughout this season of my life.

He said, "Josh, you will never have these exact emotions ever again. Capture them."

As much as I hated the idea of writing down my dark thoughts, my pain, and my emotions, I relented and took up the practice. After all, I am coachable.

I now have a journal that I've affectionately dubbed "My Pain Journal."

I can't say that I journaled every single day like I was instructed. I wrote down things that triggered my emotions.

Things that helped me early on were questions from my kids.

"Daddy, why are your eyes wet?" —Camden (age four at the time)

"Daddy, why aren't you in your work clothes?" —Harper (age eight at the time)

"Did you get fired from your job, Daddy?" —Kensington (age six at the time)

The sting of those questions hurt so badly that it's hard to describe. They were like sticking a knife into an already open wound. I didn't know how to answer because I was still searching for so many answers myself.

What do you wake up for when what you thought you were waking up for gets ripped away from you?

> Journal Entry – Monday, June 21, 2021 (five days after my termination and also Jenna's and my wedding anniversary)
>
> "It's Monday. I love Mondays. I know most people dread them, but I don't. A fresh start to a new week. The day to get your week started on the right foot, new opportunities, new ways, and new days to impact people. But this Monday is different. It's the first Monday since I was terminated. It was really hard to get out of bed today. Really hard! My purpose was taken from me. My people all had to show up and try to carry on their work as if nothing had changed, but in fact, everything has changed . . . at least for me. In an instant, without warning, and as cold as the Arctic Circle. My people don't deserve this. They deserve to work without fear and uncertainty. They deserve to fulfill their dreams without this giant distraction. One of the things that hurts the most is that I'm not there to comfort or protect them right now. I continue to pray, know, and have faith in God's plan, but I cannot help myself from asking . . . why?"

My shortest journal entry turned out to be my most powerful. It was two words: "They're watching!"

At the time, I was talking about my kids, but it turns out that everyone was. My wife, my former team, my community, and even my haters.

They wanted to see if I would curl up in a ball and remain defeated after getting kicked down so badly, OR if I would rise again like a phoenix from the ashes.

> Journal Entry: "GET UP! Know who your worth is in the hands of! Move forward with grace in your heart and zest in your eyes!"

We all must face this choice at some point in our lives. None of us gets out of life completely unscathed. We will all get knocked down to the point that getting up is the last thing we want to do.

We *get to* make the choice between playing the victim or the victor.

Do you know how tempting and easy it would've been to take a big buyout on the company and live a life under the radar after being publicly humiliated like that?

No one would've blamed me, BUT no one would've respected or admired me either.

Least of all myself!

> Journal Entry: "Sometimes, I have the thought that I regret putting myself 100 percent into it, but then I think about all the blessings that came from it, the people's lives I touched and changed, and the experiences I wouldn't have had without that effort.
>
> How do I move forward strategically while keeping vengeful thoughts out of my head and heart?"

Those two words, "they're watching," became my rallying cry. They drove me to determine my next step.

Notice that I did not say "steps." I said "step." When you're in this dark of a place, you cannot see the trees or the forest in front of your face. You can only singularly focus on your next step.

> Lesson: Journaling is a powerful tool for all seasons of life. According to a study in *Behavior Therapy* in 2006 by Elizabeth M. Gortner, Susan S. Rude, and James W. Pennebaker, journaling reduces symptoms of depression in individuals with Major Depressive Disorder. It aids individuals in processing difficult emotions and identifying positive aspects of their lives, which counteract negative thinking patterns.

Journaling isn't just an anecdotal practice—it has measurable effects on mental, emotional, and even physical well-being. It is effective because it engages both our minds and our emotions in a focused and intentional way.

CHAPTER 9

The Spiritual Awakening

When you're in a dark spot and emotionally distraught, it is easy to say "no" to things and become more reclusive. I did the exact opposite, partly because I was going batty not being of service to the world, but also because I wanted to keep myself open to life. I couldn't let this fall beat me. Remember, "they're watching"!

I said "yes" to as many things as possible. If you needed someone to golf with, I was there. If you wanted to grab lunch, I'd be happy to. If you wanted to grab a cigar after work, I was your Huckleberry.

A good friend called me one day and told me he knew of a "Spiritual Healer" that he'd done some work with before. To say this was out of my comfort zone would have been an understatement. I'm a devout Christian, and I put my faith in God and God's Word.

I wasn't into the "woo woo" world of spirituality. Crystals and astrological signs are not something I believe in, but for some reason, my curiosity got the best of me. I asked him some more questions about what that entails and his previous experiences with the person.

After talking with Jenna about it, I decided to give it a whirl. I was desperate for some answers and needed healing.

Before going to see this Spiritual Healer, I did more research, specifically on Ketamine Therapy. I found a mountain of stories and testimonials, ranging from our military veterans to everyday people who suffered from PTSD, depression, anxiety, and a slew of other ailments.

Almost all of their stories told of positive outcomes after their therapy sessions. It was time for me to lean in and give it a shot (literally and metaphorically).

I showed up that day with mixed feelings of excitement and apprehension. My friend joined me to introduce me to the Spiritual Healer and bring me some comfort before my journey.

I could sense right away why my friend trusted her. She had such a calming, spiritual nature about her. I still had zero clue what I was in for, but I felt comfortable with her presence.

We exchanged some small talk, and I asked her more about what I should expect. She told me that everyone's experience is different based on what they're bringing mentally and emotionally with them that day.

I said, "Well, I'm a mess, so I'm a bit nervous about what's going to come up for me."

She once again assured me that she'd be with me every step of the way.

I was ready to begin.

I gave her my pain journal, and she gave me a sleep mask. She turned on some music. I have very little recollection of what was playing, but she was limiting some of my senses to work inward.

The best way I can describe my experience is in three distinct phases.

The Past.
The Present.
The Future.

In round one, my past came up, but it had nothing to do with work. I had visions of my grandparents. It was like they were right there with me, even though all of my grandparents were deceased at this point.

I could hear their voices as plain as day. I could see their smiles. They told me how proud they were of me.

I even had a vision of an old Indian chief. Now, this may seem random, but let me explain. My paternal grandparents' house was located right at the base of a place in Ottawa, IL, called Starved Rock, a famous landmark where two rival Indian tribes feuded, and one of the tribes starved the other and threw them into the Illinois River.

My grandparents' house was rumored (never confirmed) to be on an old Indian burial ground. Even if it wasn't, they weren't far off because I found old arrowheads in the dirt when I was a kid.

I had a recurring dream every single time I slept at their home. I would fall through the bed I was sleeping in into the basement bedroom and find myself sitting across a fire from an old Indian chief with no shirt, face painted, and full headdress.

As a kid, this scared the living daylights out of me. It was a nightmare every time.

In my dream, I would sprint as fast as I could away from him, and if I could get up the stairs and jump across a gap in the floor and into the living room where my grandparents were drinking coffee and reading the newspaper, the dream would end. If the Indians caught me, I'd stay in the nightmare.

This vision showed me that exact same Indian chief with no shirt, face painted, and full headdress of feathers, but this time, I wasn't scared. He was there with me and brought me a calm and caring presence.

The past brought me calm, peace, and joy. It was so nice to see and hear all of my grandparents, their smiles, and their pride in me.

It was like I had one last moment with them all over again.

In round two, my mind shifted to the present.

My visions focused on my family, my four kids, and my wife, Jenna.

In this round, I remember squeezing the pillow the Healer had for me so tightly. My sleep mask still on, my mind was fully on my family. I was rolling on the ground playing with my kids, hearing them laugh, and smiling so BIG! Just fully immersed in the moment with them.

My wife was on the couch, smiling and appreciating the love between me and the kids as we played. I don't know if I have ever felt such love as I did in that moment. Happy tears flooded my eyes, and I was just there . . . in love!

I really didn't want to leave this moment. It was an overwhelming feeling. My whole body felt euphoric.

In round three, my mind again shifted, and this time, it was future-oriented.

My head had already been in the space of moving on from the financial industry. I was leaning into coaching entrepreneurs and leadership teams on a big scale. However, Jenna didn't want me on the road all of the time as a speaker and coach. Considering we were raising four young kids, that was a more than reasonable request as I planned out our future.

Back in my session, my mind was in a dreamscape that I hadn't experienced before. For the first time since my termination, I was able to dream about the future. I started to envision open land, trees, and water—a place where people could get away from their computer screens and out from under their fluorescent lights.

Then, it hit me.

I had a *Field of Dreams* moment.

"If you build it, they will come."

Build a place where people can disconnect from the hustle and bustle of their daily lives, detach, and work inward.

A place where people can get out of their business to work on their business.

A place where people can get out of their lives to work on their lives.

A place for community and connection.

A sanctuary for personal and professional development.

This place wouldn't be like any other. I'd create a space for spiritual, physical, mental, and emotional growth and healing as well as relationship enrichment, experiential learning, fun, exploration, and, of course, we'd work on business and financial abundance and growth.

I would build a zen garden with a tiny chapel for worship that is welcoming for all religious beliefs. There would also be a separate garden to grow and share vegetables, fruits, and spices. And of course, there would be plenty of animals to graze, create a friendly presence, and make people smile.

In short, I would build a place where you could experience joy, freedom, and health so that you could go back to your world to create more success and significance.

Every fiber of my being could envision what I wanted to build. My purpose was restored, and I could see something I could run towards again.

I had a mission again!

Then, my Healer took off my sleep mask and welcomed me back to the present. I was still out of it, but my whole body and mind felt amazing.

She gave me some water, and I started to talk about how I felt.

I remember asking her how she experienced me during the session.

She responded, "You processed a TON of grief."

I said, "But I felt blissful and happy the whole time, why is that?"

She told me, "We have to process our grief to get to a newfound peace."

That statement was and is profound.

I had been going through the five stages of grief (denial, anger, bargaining, depression, and acceptance). I was in the depression stage. Going through this spiritual experience was moving me towards acceptance.

> (Disclaimer: I am not advocating that anyone go through Ketamine Therapy. I'm simply sharing my experience. That being said, I've had numerous friends who have gone through Ayahuasca ceremonies, Ibogaine, Bufo (toad medicine), Psilocybin, and more for their traumas and their own life journey. All have had their own positive experiences and healing. I do believe in alternative plant medicine and also believe it's a deeply personal decision.)

CHAPTER 10

The New Mission

That spiritual journey was on a Friday. On Monday the following week, I called a realtor friend of mine and told him I was looking for 80 to 100 acres of land.

I shared with him a brief version of my vision and told him to narrow his search to within a forty-five-minute radius of our airport, as I didn't want people who came to see me to fly in and then have to drive another long distance.

Only one problem: I didn't have the money for the land purchase at this time because my negotiation with my former company was still dragging on.

Nevertheless, my realtor and I went shopping. We found properties that had many structures, trees, valleys, and rolling hills. We found other properties that were nothing but blank slates, and I would envision what I would have to build to fulfill my new dream. My realtor and I would debrief after visiting each listing so I could share what I liked and disliked about each property to help him better refine his search.

Then, one day, a great friend, Joe, paid me a visit at my home. Joe and I have been friends for over twenty years. He's one of those friends that you don't see very often, but when you do, you pick up right where you left off.

Joe wanted to check in on me as a good friend does, as he knew I was going through it. We got to catch up on all things in my world and his. I decided to share my new vision with him, which I had only done with my wife and my realtor up to this point. I was keeping it close to the vest while

I was still in those negotiations, but for some reason, I felt compelled to share it with Joe.

As he listened, he got a big smile on his face. He was not only excited for me, but I could tell he also had something to share.

He said, "Bro, have you seen this place?"

He then turned around his phone and showed me a video of this majestic property with acres of woods with deer strolling through them, a large rustic barn, a brand new modern home, a newly built horse arena, a stream through the middle of it (which appeased my water requirement), and so much more.

My jaw dropped, and I had butterflies in my stomach. I asked him where it was, and to my surprise, it was located just outside of Madison—only a twelve-minute drive to downtown and less than twenty minutes to the airport.

I asked, "Where did you find this?"

I asked because it wasn't listed on the Multiple Listing Service.

I cannot remember how he learned of the property, but he had been exploring land with his girlfriend, a therapist, to host retreats. I got the link from Joe and forwarded it to my realtor, instructing him to get us a showing.

The very next week, we were on this majestic property.

When I arrived, the listing agent asked me to sign an NDA (non-disclosure agreement). I thought this was odd as I was coming to view a property and had never been asked to do that before. Being curious, I asked why.

The listing agent simply responded, "The owner is very private."

To which I replied, "Since I'm signing this, may I ask who the owner is?"

The listing agent told me. Not only did I know the owner, he constructed Jenna's and my first home.

Now, I've always said, "Madison, WI, is only one degree of separation." But this was straight out of God's blueprint.

Jenna and I bought our first home in 2008. For those of you old enough to remember, that was the absolute worst time to buy a brand-new home. The market crashed, and so did the values of homes across the country. We bought at the peak of the market.

The home we built was part of a large development with condominiums and townhomes in downtown Madison. The owner of the property I was viewing happened to be the developer of this large project. He lived in the penthouse with his wife, while we lived downstairs in one of the three-story townhomes.

Because of the timing, nearly 75 percent of the condos and homes were vacant since many people had bailed on their builds.

Jenna and the developer's wife spent many evenings out exercising the dogs in the open grass behind the complex. We got to know each other pretty well during that period, but we hadn't seen each other in about seven years since we moved to the suburbs after having our second child.

Back to the property.

My realtor and I got a tour of the house, the barn, and the horse arena.

Afterwards, we debriefed as we always did, and I let him know it's not exactly what I would've built in my vision, but it checks a LOT of the boxes.

I could see small retreats and dinners being held at home and bigger retreats, bourbon tastings, and speaking events in the large barn. The more I spoke, the more I liked not having to build everything from scratch, taking what was existing and just making it better to fulfill the vision.

When we asked for another showing, I also requested that the owner be there. Seeing my old friend again was even more special as he personally took me on an ATV tour of the entire eighty acres.

He explained the property's history. Amazingly, when he purchased it, it was held in trust by the fifth generation of a family who had owned it for over 140 years.

When he arrived on-site to view the property, the barn was about to collapse, the driveway was a dirt road, and the farmhouse was decrepit. He built a modern home to offset the old, rugged feel of the old barn and grainery. Instead of tearing down the large barn that was tipping over, he chose to restore and reinforce it. There was even a very modern treehouse in the woods that he built for his grandchildren, where they could spend the night under the stars.

He also enclosed the entire eighty acres with five-foot-tall black horse fencing. I couldn't even imagine how long and tedious that project was.

The land was so overgrown that he had to do a lot of tree removal and even brought in 300 goats to clear away much of the undergrowth. I didn't know that was a thing, but apparently, you can hire people with herds of goats to do this for you.

As we finalized the more extensive tour, he invited me to sit down on the back patio for a conversation. We shared a glass of bourbon and talked about life as well as my vision. I told him about what happened to me and the fallout of my forced exit from my previous company.

He is a man of God also. He looked at me and said, "You know, Josh, God's not done with you yet."

I said, "I know, and that's why I'm leaning into this vision He has for me now."

He said, "Why don't you bring your wife and kids out next. For a big decision like this, I know they should be a part of it."

He was right.

It was also a clever sales tactic as he knew that as soon as my wife and kids saw this slice of Heaven, they'd fall in love with it as well. It didn't matter what the intentions were; I was so excited to get them out there that I took him up on the offer, and we came back the next week.

This time, he gave me the keys to the ATV and told me to show them around.

I took my kids up to the treehouse, and they immediately started fighting over who got to swing on the swing first. When we got back up to the house, they were running through the large lawn and asking to go see the horses and donkeys.

The asking price on this property was not a small number. In fact, no property that I looked at had a small asking price. Land is expensive. It doesn't matter if there are dwellings, buildings, or just a blank slate . . . you're going to pay a big number for land.

We sat on the back patio again, conversing. I told him I had fallen in love with the property and could see my vision coming to life. The problem was still the problem. My negotiations weren't done, and I had no idea when they would come to a close. Therefore, I had no money to put in a meaningful offer to him.

I swallowed my pride and said, "I know the money is coming, I just have no idea when. I thought this exit and negotiation would've finalized months ago."

Then, something amazing happened—a true blessing.

He said, "Josh, I love your vision for this place. I put in a lot of hard work to make this what it is, and it's time for me to downsize my life and move on. Not only do I love your vision, I trust you. If you say the money is coming, I trust you that the money is coming. So, how about this, how about we do an interest-only land contract for a year? Do you think the money will be here within the next year?"

I said, "God, I hope so."

He is an astute and skilled businessman. There's no doubt he's had his share of wins, losses, and lawsuits as all business owners do, but he said two extremely powerful things to me that made me feel humbled and seen at the same time.

"I believe in your vision."

"I trust you."

As a leader, as a man, those are two of the most empowering sentences you can ever say to another human being.

He did say one other thing, "I don't want a bunch of back and forth between our realtors. You come up with a number and call me directly. You and I will work this out."

I had a directive, and now, I had my next steps.

I began to place pressure on my attorney to bring our negotiations with my former company to a close.

I also did my research by assessing other properties. The day before Thanksgiving 2021, we came to a mutually agreeable number and informed the realtors to get to work to bring the deal to a close.

CHAPTER 11

Hard Reset: How 75 Days of Pain Rewired My Mind, Body, and Vision

The holiday season is busy for everyone, especially if you have kids. The holiday season of 2021 was particularly busy for us. Beyond the presents for the kids and seeing family, we had two closings.

On December 29, 2021, we finally negotiated and signed my exit with my former company. That chapter of my life had finally come to a close, and it was time for me to begin my next chapter.

The very next day, on December 30, we closed on the property.

Writing that large check was monumental, but the blessing and opportunity to grow into this vision I had felt was momentous—a true Kairos moment.

I pulled into the long driveway of our new eighty-acre farm on January 2, 2022. There was snow on the ground, and the sun was shining off the bright white snow.

I decided to get my phone out and record a video of me pulling up the driveway and to the house. I posted that video on my social media with the words: "I can't wait to share with the world my vision for this place."

I sat in my office (the old grainery) on the old architectural draft desk and a chair the previous owner left, not knowing exactly what to do. I am a high-level visionary. I can see the big picture, I can see the goals, and even some of the steps to take, but details and organization ... not in my wheelhouse.

Although I was free from one legal battle with my previous company, the other lawsuit pending against me still cast a dark cloud over my head, as I still had to resolve the issue with Richard. On top of that, my psyche and mental health had been through the ringer over the past six months.

In order for me to build a brand new business, get it off the ground, and start marching towards that vision I imagined, I desperately needed a mental reboot. I had to get my "killer instinct" back, that young and ambitious mind that climbed previous mountains and overcame many obstacles.

Insert 75 Hard.

For those living under a rock who haven't heard of the world's most popular mental toughness training program created by one of my mentors, Andy Frisella, it goes like this ...

For seventy-five straight days, you have to complete these tasks daily without exception and ZERO compromises.

1. Two forty-five-minute workouts—one of which must be outdoors
2. Follow a structured diet—no cheat meals and no alcohol
3. Drink one gallon of water
4. Read ten pages in a non-fiction book
5. Take a progress picture

I was already in pretty good shape, but I wasn't doing this to get in great shape physically. I needed to get my *mind* back in shape.

I embarked on my first 75 Hard journey on January 17, 2022.

On the very first day, I slipped on the stairs at the farmhouse and messed up my shin and foot. It was like the universe was testing me to see if I was really going through with this.

A week in, my feet were killing me. I was trekking through a foot of snow in boots for my outdoor workouts, but those boots were not meant for hiking. If I had gone to see a doctor, the diagnosis would've certainly been bone spurs.

I decided that I had to invest in some new footwear and keep the train moving.

The hardest part for me at first wasn't the two workouts or the reading. I've been in the habit of working out most days of the week, and since adulthood, I've been an avid self-development reader.

No, the hardest part initially was the gallon of water and giving up my nightcap . . . my pour of rare and expensive bourbon.

The number of times you pee each day when you're properly hydrated is something to get used to, and I did over time.

On Day 24, I fell on some ice and hurt my leg, but not badly enough to quit.

I battled a sinus infection from Days 26 through 31. Once I got over that illness, I began really hitting my groove.

On Day 40, I had an epiphany that has changed my life.

While on my daily ruck through the snow, I thought to myself, "Forty days without a drop of alcohol. Have I ever done that?

"I've done 'Sober October' and 'Dry January' before, but those are just thirty-one days respectively. Even during my college football days, we'd work out hard and then go party. I hadn't gone forty days entirely dry since I was seventeen years old, and I am currently forty-one years old.

"How sad is that?!"

This thought train fundamentally changed how I viewed the role of alcohol in my life. I live in Wisconsin. There are studies done yearly, and the last one I saw said, "Of the 50 drunkest counties in the United States, 44 of them are located in Wisconsin."

Alcohol is the culture in the state of Wisconsin. We're known for beer, cheese, and brats. That is an excuse for all of us that becomes our reality. I've always been more of a contrarian thinker, and this way of life just doesn't fit my future reality.

My goal is to be the very best me for my family and the clients I'm privileged to serve. I cannot fulfill that mission when I drink alcohol. Even if I have one drink, I am not as mentally sharp the next day. When you're free of artificial sugars and alcohol for forty straight days, the level of clarity you have in your mind is nothing short of astounding.

Seriously, if you haven't done this, I highly encourage you to give it a try. Even if you can't get onboard with 75 Hard yet, going free from processed sugars and alcohol creates an environment for your mind the way God intended it to be.

Clear.
Focused.
Full of imagination.

I gave serious contemplation to giving up alcohol forever. I spent the next thirty days tossing this around in my head. I didn't have an addiction like many friends of mine have had. I had a relationship with alcohol. I really enjoy fine and rare bourbon. I love the hunt of it and enjoy the fruits of that labor.

What I came to is this, I didn't want to neglect myself a celebration or special event. I don't drink unless I'm with special people or at special events. Now I realize that you could justify in your mind that a lot of things are special events.

That was not my decision. To put it in perspective, I had less than thirty drinks total in that year.

Day 45, I wrote in my journal, "I could do this forever!" Then Day 55 happened.

It was supposed to be a seamless day, but it turned out to be the exact opposite.

We were headed to West Palm Beach for spring break as a family. We had a connection in Detroit, and we found out as soon as we landed that our flight to Florida had been cancelled due to weather down there.

The problem was that I was counting on landing in Florida at 1 p.m. and getting both workouts done there. Now, we were stuck in Detroit with four young kids and no luggage.

We had to figure out our hotel room for the night, our flight to be rebooked, clothing, food, and every other unexpected detail. A new challenge and problem to solve.

After we got our hotel room (thank God that the hotel inside DTW had a room for us) and our flight rebooked, we decided to Uber to Target. I had to buy outdoor clothes (it was 15 degrees outside) and indoor workout clothes.

When we returned, Jenna got the kids fed, and I headed outside to the parking ramp for my first workout of the day at 4:30 p.m.

The air traffic control tower must've been laughing at me as I was parading around on the top of the ramp for about an hour, but I was laughing as well because I felt so empowered that very few people would've been this committed to getting an outdoor workout in the freezing cold while they were supposed to be in Florida on their vacation.

This is one of the key mental toughness foundations that 75 Hard provides if you do the program correctly. When you commit, you are choosing to do something very few people on the planet will ever attempt. Most will call you crazy, while others will say, "I could never do that."

For those that do, you realize you are not normal. You are one of the few who choose to be uncommon amongst the common. You begin to relish these difficult times and the bad weather. You wear them as badges of honor.

I finished my indoor workout around 9:30 p.m. and went to bed to catch that early flight to Florida.

There is a rule that your workouts cannot be consecutive and should be spaced at least three hours apart. The reason: It's supposed to be inconvenient. The program is meant to test you mentally and physically. We all lead busy lives, and the point is to stretch what you think you are capable of.

One of the most memorable parts of my already special vacation with my family was learning I didn't need to drink at all to have fun with those I love. In fact, it made me more present and more fun as I wasn't worried about getting the next cocktail from the poolside server.

On Day 72, I completed 111 push-ups in 60 seconds after an upper-body workout. I had transformed into pure beast mode.

On Day 74, I wrote this in my journal:

> Arthritis in my knee was flaring during my leg workout, but we worked through it. This has been an unforgettable journey. I'm so happy I chose to embark on it, and with one day to go, I'm very proud of myself. Someone would have to kill me to not finish tomorrow. You could chop off my leg, and I'll army crawl outside for 45 minutes. I cannot be stopped!

On Day 75, I soaked up every minute of every task. I was relishing all that I had been through over the last seventy-five days. Three head colds, bone spurs, hemorrhoids, planes, trains, automobiles, and everything in between.

The amount of pride, joy, and sense of fulfillment I had lying my head down at night on Day 75 is something I'll remember forever.

75 Hard did exactly what I needed it to do for my mental game and more!

I was back.

Not only did I have my mind back, but my body was in as good shape as when I was playing football back in college. I measured in at 208 pounds and eight percent body fat.

With my mojo clearly back, I was ready to attack this new vision.

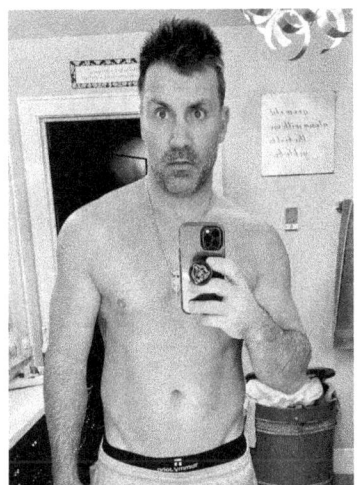 

Before   After

CHAPTER 12

From Idols to Impact

The property I purchased was given a name by the previous owner. He installed five bridges on the property to traverse different parts of the land, as a couple of streams run through it.

I kept the name. Not because I was in love with the reason he named it that, but because I had an idea that had far more symbolism to my journey and the gift that I wanted to give back to the world.

You see, when I was in my pit of despair and during those evenings spent by my fire pit alone in thought, I was beginning to understand where I had gone wrong over the years. I spent the majority of my adult life and career chasing down goals, money, and professional accolades.

I was idolizing all the wrong things.

The Bible is explicitly clear. In fact, one of the Ten Commandments, as found in Exodus 20:3-5, is: "You shall have no other gods (idols) before me."

Most of society looks at this commandment and thinks about false gods. Perhaps you think of Zeus or other Ancient Greek mythology, but that's not the whole message God is trying to convey. We have plenty of idols in our lives that we place before God. He is talking about any idol, be it material, ideological, or spiritual.

Here's a short list of my idols at the time.

- ✓ The company that I represented
- ✓ My position
- ✓ My accolades
- ✓ Money

For you, it might be your spouse, your kids, or your possessions.

Anything can become an idol if you place more importance on that thing or person than on your relationship with God. I had to take stock of my wrongs and get right with Him.

Then, one day after my forced exit, the boxes arrived at my home. My former company hired professional movers to clean out my old office, box it all up, and deliver those boxes to my home. It took me a while to open them, but once I did, I felt an overwhelming sense of discontent.

It wasn't because I missed my old life, but rather that I missed the mark in my old life so badly. I had the awakening that all of the trophies, ribbons, certifications, and professional designations only meant something to me.

My office was filled with books, plaques, designation certificates, and awards that all gave the impression that I was credible, professional, and successful.

These things were my idols.

There wasn't a single thing in those boxes that I couldn't do without.

There wasn't a single thing in those boxes that could go with me to Heaven.

Worse yet, I started to question what it was all for.

I knew that in my position at the time, I could be replaced if I wasn't doing the job, but I never once considered that I could be replaced while doing the job very well.

> Lesson: Everyone is replaceable . . . even you!

My questions persisted, and they got more painful for me to recognize my wrongs.

"Did I chase God with the same determination and persistence that I did my goals and ambitions?"

"Did I pursue my wife with the same passion and fortitude that I did my vision for business?"

"Did I dedicate as much time and attention to my kids as I did my career?"

"Did I prioritize my mental and physical health to the degree I prioritized my work schedule?"

The hard truth: My answer was "no" to ALL of those questions.

That rocked me in such a profound way. When you get kicked down as hard and as publicly as I did, it is extremely lonely.

You feel as if there is nothing left.

I lost everything professionally, but thank God, I didn't lose the people I cared about most in this world. They were right there with me in my pit of despair. They loved me just the same.

My wife was uncertain about what was next, but she didn't love me any less.

My kids loved that I was around more with them, and they couldn't care less what my "job" was; they still loved me the same.

Just when I felt I had nothing, I realized I had everything I ever needed and more. Although I was feeling deep remorse and gratitude seemingly simultaneously, I didn't have much time before the next questions popped into my brain.

"What if I got it all wrong? What if we all have it wrong?"

When you were a kid, do you remember being asked the question, "What do you want to be when you grow up?"

You may have even asked your kids the same question. It's a question that has seemingly been passed down from one generation to the next. Some parents even wear it as a badge of honor as they tout, "Well, my kid wants to be a doctor when he grows up."

I never had an answer to that question other than I wanted to play in the NFL. Again, I wasn't good enough to fulfill that dream, and I never had a backup plan.

But then that question gets reinforced in high school as our teachers and counselors ask us what we want to major in college. Once we're in college, we're constantly asked what we plan to do with our degree after graduation (or if we even graduate).

Everyone is focused on the "what." We don't realize as a society that we're framing our existence. It's like the same lame question every time you go to a networking event: "What do you do?"

It's a question to measure someone up. "Are they important or worth your time?" type-of-question.

Here's a better question for us adults to ask children or the next generation: "Who do you want to be when you grow up?"

No one ever stops to ask us, "Who do you want to be, and why do you want to be it?"

The "who" is far more important than the "what."

I'd be lying if I said we haven't asked our children the "what" question, but I'm far more concerned with the "who." Jenna and I are raising our kids to be great humans first. Humans who are kind and resilient, empathetic and loving, determined, and with high integrity. Humans who love God and follow His Word.

There is plenty of wiggle room for success in that frame. After all, success can be measured in a variety of ways.

We've all met highly successful individuals who have lost their way with their spouse, their kids, or their health.

We've seen highly successful individuals numb their stress in unhealthy ways through alcohol, drugs, gambling, or pornography.

There's more to life than our career success and our bank accounts. Most of us know this, even if just deep down. The problem is recognizing it and living it out with all the demands on our shoulders in this world.

I was blessed to not only be kicked off the mountain top but also to be given these six months to heal, redesign my vision, and learn the lessons God was teaching me.

Once you learn your lessons and determine your gifts from God, the next step is realizing they weren't just for you.

I believe it's our job to learn our gifts and our lessons so we can put them in service for others. Our gifts weren't meant for us! They were given to us to steward and give back to the world.

I learned through my forced exit that there was a gift in my pain. You see, sometimes, God's preparation is packaged in pain.

I had to go through that pit of despair to learn very valuable lessons, and because I chose to face my pain, I came out the other side of it with lessons to give back to the world.

Our world needs healing.

We are overworked, overburdened, and disconnected from what matters most.

We're married to our screens instead of our families.

We're trapped inside instead of exploring the magnificence God gave us outside.

We eat foods that are poisoning us instead of foods that nourish us.

We cannot heal the world without first healing ourselves.

No politician is going to save us.

It's on each one of us to buck the norm.
It's on each one of us to take back what God gave to us.
To live a righteous life devoted to Him.
To provide and protect.
To love and behold our families and other cherished relationships.
To be the very best versions of ourselves so we can give our best selves to others.

The events that took place that led me to these conclusions and what I'm about to teach you were some of the most excruciating emotional pain one can go through. I wouldn't wish it upon my worst enemy.
AND
Because of these hardships and my decision to walk the dark, lonely path, I found enlightenment that I feel needs to be shared with the world, deep in my soul.
I began piecing together the "integrated life."
That was my initial title or thesis.
What did it mean to live an integrated life?
As I said before, I don't believe in a "balanced life" only because of the connotation it presents. Most people think of "balance" as 50/50. We will never achieve a 50/50 work/life balance, but we can achieve work/life integration or harmony.
I've long been a fan of Darren Hardy's "Wheel of Life."
On his wheel, he separates:

- Financial
- Business
- Lifestyle
- Mental
- Spiritual
- Family

- Relationships
- Physical

You answer questions on an assessment and then place your dots to see if your wheel is "balanced" or lopsided.

I've done that exercise at least once a year for over a decade. I found one problem with it, though. There was no order to his spokes on the wheel.

Everything I just went through the past six months taught me there is a proper order to those things, and most of us (including me) screw that order up. Someone may not place lifestyle or business as high importance in their lives as family and spirituality.

As I was thinking about my lessons learned, I was also building out my coaching framework for the clients I worked with.

Darren Hardy's Wheel of Life kept coming to mind, but I was still unsettled with the order and not placing equal importance on each item based on everything I had just been through.

Then, it came to me.

If I'm not right with God, who has given me life on this earth, then nothing else matters.

Spirituality has to come first.

Now, you may not believe what I believe, and I'm not here to preach to you, but I'm certain you've been to a visitation or a funeral in your lifetime. And if you have, you know that while the body is there, the soul and the spirit are gone. Knowing this, we can only draw one conclusion: Regardless of whether you share my Christian belief, we can agree that we're spiritual beings. Therefore, we must guard and tend our spiritual life first and foremost above anything else.

Just like that, The Spiritual Bridge[IP] was born.

As I looked at the Wheel of Life again and assessed what was to come next, I realized that a couple of them belonged together.

Every time we board an airplane, a flight attendant gets on the intercom and instructs us with a very key directive: "In case of emergency, oxygen masks will drop. Please put your oxygen mask on FIRST before assisting others."

They always say it so nicely, but it's not a suggestion; it's a directive.

Why?

Because we cannot assist anyone else if we're passed out or dead, in order for us to be our very best for others in our lives, we must be our very best for ourselves first.

Our mental, emotional, and physical health must be a point of emphasis in our daily lives.

The second bridge, The Internal Bridge[IP], encompasses all of the hard work we must do on ourselves internally to become the best outward-facing human we could be.

As I dug deeper into my lessons, one thing became clear.

When I was down in the pits of my despair and at my lowest point, Jesus was right there with me. He wasn't missing in action, and He wasn't above me to pull me up; He walked alongside me every step of the way. In addition, my wife, my kids, and my extended family never wavered in their love and support for me.

Most of the people we interact with on a day-to-day basis won't care enough to be at our funerals. They may not even give it a second thought when they hear word that we passed away, but I sure hope that we're blessed enough to have those we loved the most there in our last moments and at our funerals.

Relationships matter, and the order of which relationship we focus on first matters.

1. God
2. Yourself
3. Your spouse (if you have one)

4. Your children (if you have them)
5. Everyone else

Our job is to NOT mess up the order!

As you may have guessed, this leads to The Relationship Bridge^{IP}.

The path was so abundantly clear to me that I felt like a fool for not recognizing it sooner in my life.

The vast majority of our adult lives, we spend working and saving or investing for a day when we no longer have to work. I loved helping people retire before they thought they could. It would bring me such joy to present a financial plan that showed them that, based on their great savings and investing habits, they could retire sooner than expected.

But I also met with plenty of people who didn't have great habits and were essentially on a path to never be able to retire, or at the very least, to live a very different lifestyle if they did.

We should love our work because we spend so much of our lives in our work.

As Colossians 3:23-24 says, "Whatever you do, work at it with all your heart, as working for the Lord, not for human masters, since you know that you will receive an inheritance from the Lord as a reward. It is the Lord Christ you are serving."

Our next step is The Environment Bridge^{IP}, as it is the environment you create for your life, encompassing your professional, financial, and creative lives. This is the Bridge that everyone jumps to immediately because they are focused on their professional endeavors. This is what society tells us is the most important thing to focus on.

If we get these four Bridges right and in the correct order, we can leave an incredible mark on the world. We create a ripple effect that reverberates through time.

One of my favorite quotes of all time came from my favorite hip-hop artist of all time, Tupac Shakur: "I'm not saying I'm gonna change the world, but I guarantee that I will spark the brain that will change the world."

That's my hope with my words in this book.

When most people think about the word "Legacy," they think about inheritance and what is left behind when someone passes away. In actuality, "what" is left behind is of little consequence after losing a loved one. Most people would give all the money and possessions back to the world just to have one more day, one more hug, one more "I love you" from their loved one that passed.

Legacy is NOT what we leave behind. Legacy is what we leave IN people.

It's the impact we had while we were on this earth. It's how we helped others. It's how we made others feel in our presence. It's the gifts and lessons we bestowed on those we had the opportunity to impact.

The Legacy Bridge[IP] is last, and it is my belief that we only leave an amazing legacy IF we get the proper order to the first four Bridges correct.

5 Bridges Farm may have been named by the previous owner because it has five physical bridges, but now the farm and those bridges have a whole new meaning.

Before We Begin: What's the Gap Between the Life You Have . . . and the Life You're Called to Live?

Most people *feel* the disconnect, but few know how to define it, let alone align with purpose across every area of life.

That's why I created the **Life Quotient Assessment**[IP], a powerful, personal tool to help you measure what truly matters before we explore how to transform it.

I highly encourage you to take the assessment prior to reading Part Two of this book to get a baseline understanding of the life you are currently leading versus the life you were meant to live.

Here's what it does:

It evaluates how aligned you are across the **5 Bridges of Kairos**.

Your personalized scorecard will give you:

- An overall **Life Quotient Score**
- Individual scores across each Bridge
- A snapshot of where you're thriving and where you're drifting
- A baseline to measure real, lasting growth

Before we dive into the framework that can *transform everything*...

Take the Life Quotient Assessment now!

Scan the QR code or visit joshkosnick.com/assessment to get your custom report.

Because awareness is the first bridge to alignment.

Let's start this journey with clarity—and end it with transformation.

PART TWO
THE 5 BRIDGES OF KAIROS

CHAPTER 13

The Spiritual Bridge
(The Unconscious Being and Metaphysical)

February 7, 2018

I rushed home from the office to pack for vacation.

Every year, we'd take our top advisors and their spouses on an awards trip somewhere tropical in the middle of winter to celebrate the previous year's success.

That year, we were headed to Mexico.

In typical fashion, I hadn't packed a thing, and we were set to depart for Chicago that evening to fly out of O'Hare in the morning. I was frantically getting my bags packed and making sure that I didn't forget anything, so my cell phone wasn't even on my radar.

Camden (our youngest) was seven months old at the time. Jenna was busy feeding him and trying to get him down for a nap before we had to leave. By the time I picked up my cell again, I had missed several calls and texts, all of them from various family members of Jenna's.

I listened to one of the voicemails. It was from Jenna's aunt. Her voice quivered, urging me to call her back immediately.

My stomach sank to the floor. I knew something was really wrong.

As I hit the number to call her back, I was expecting the worst and praying for the best. I honestly couldn't tell you what I thought the "worst" was, but it certainly wasn't as bad as it actually was.

When I reached her, she could barely get the words out. "Josh, Tom shot himself. He's gone."

Not only was my stomach on the floor now, but my heart was there as well.

My wife's dad, my father-in-law, my kids' grandfather, my friend, and my spiritual mentor was gone at just fifty-eight years old.

I immediately went out into our garage so that neither my kids nor my wife could find me sobbing. I wasn't ready to utter those words out loud yet.

I called my COO (Chief Operations Officer), who was on her way to our home to ride with us down to Chicago. I had to tell her we couldn't go on the trip.

I could barely speak.

I gathered myself briefly to move to our basement, another spot where I wouldn't easily be found. I called my mom, who was supposed to be on her way over to watch the kids, but she didn't answer.

I got hold of my dad, who was up north at our family's lake home. I told him the news with tears streaming down my face. There aren't any right words in a situation like this, but he did his best to comfort me.

Part of my pain was that I knew what I had to do next.

I had to tell my wife the hardest thing I've ever had to tell her.

I vulnerably confided in my dad, "I don't know what to do. I don't know how to tell her."

He just said, "You need your Mom there. I'll get a hold of her and see how far away she is."

I somehow cleared the visible tears from my face and mustered the courage to go upstairs to our bedroom.

Jenna was still breastfeeding Cam and trying to get him to sleep. I asked if I could hold him because I didn't know how she'd react to the most devastating news she's ever received.

She saw right through me.

"What's wrong?" she asked.

Then, I spoke the words I never thought I'd have to say. This was by far the most difficult conversation I've ever had to have in my entire life, and it was only one sentence.

Instead of heading to Chicago and then Mexico, we headed to Indiana to be with her family and say goodbye to one of the greatest men either of us has ever known.

Before we left for Indiana, I had one more difficult conversation to have. I sat down on the couch with my two oldest girls (Ella and Harper). Ella was seven years old, and Harper was five at the time.

I told them that Grandpa Tom died tonight. He went to be with Jesus. I couldn't tell them how he died; it was too much for those young ages to understand. They asked. Kids are far smarter than most adults want to give them credit for, but I couldn't tell them. Instead, I told them his heart stopped.

At Tom's visitation, there was a four-hour wait. It seemed that everyone who ever encountered Tom wanted to show up for the family and pay their respects. Hundreds of people from all over the country came in for his visitation and funeral. Tom made an impact with every person, business associate, and beyond.

I was one of the few chosen by my mother-in-law, Pam, to eulogize Tom. I told everyone there that the thing I was most sad about was that our four kids wouldn't get to grow up with his presence and know just how great he was.

But then I told them that's only partially true. Only if those of us that Tom impacted don't pass along those stories and lessons to them. Tom left an indelible mark on each of us, and I'm counting on all of you to pass that on to our kids, his grandkids.

Now that you've learned how my father-in-law, Tom, died, I believe it's more important for you to know how he lived and why I share this heartbreaking story with you.

Tom grew up in rural Indiana. His parents were farmers before getting into the trucking industry. The hard work he learned by farming paid dividends as he decided to embark on his entrepreneurial journey. He decided to follow in his father's footsteps into trucking, just a different lane. He sold semi-trucks wholesale.

Like all entrepreneurs, he started from the bottom and figured things out as he went.

When I first started dating Jenna in 2007, we were long-distance, and the first opportunity I had to meet both Tom and Pam was at Jenna's college graduation ceremony.

They were skeptical of me because I was not only a few years older and Jenna was their baby girl, but also because I was a couple of states away. They knew she was smitten, and that was a threat because their whole extended family lived within one square mile of each other. They didn't want her to move away.

At that point, they were already very successful in their trucking business. Tom weathered the storm as a new entrepreneur, and by 2007, he was a grizzly veteran.

When I first shook Tom's hand, I met a strong man with such a calm and kind presence.

Only one month after meeting him for the first time, I asked for his daughter's hand in marriage, or as he would tell you, I told him I was going to ask her.

I guess I was just going for the "assumed close."

Over the years, Tom not only became my father-in-law but also my friend. We spent a lot of time together talking about life, God, raising Godly kids, and cars.

He loved cars!

As a stress relief, he'd fix up old muscle cars and sell them in pristine condition. He wouldn't keep a penny for himself. All that money was given to charity.

While the girls went shopping, Tom and I would catch a movie or go to the gun range he built on some land behind their home.

I observed him faithfully read his Bible every morning, go to church every Sunday, and, most importantly, live his life in a way that honored God.

To see him light up with love and laughter around his loved ones (especially his grandkids) was truly a sight to behold. His smile and laugh were so infectious that he truly lit up the room.

He didn't know a stranger. He treated everyone with kindness and respect.

I knew of situations where he would get screwed over in business and out of a lot of money. Yet, somehow, he'd handle it with grace and turn a cheek when most of us would go full nuclear on someone.

I'd ask him questions like, "Why would you just let this go?"

His answer, "It's what God would do. Can't take it with us when we go, and relationships are worth more than money."

I had never experienced another man with such humility and grace for others. He always saw the very best in people, even when they were showing him their very worst.

When Leviticus 19:18 said, "Do not seek revenge or bear a grudge against anyone among your people, but love your neighbor as yourself," Tom took those words to heart and lived by them.

I once quipped, "I don't think I've ever heard Tom raise his voice."

I was quickly corrected by both my wife and mother-in-law that he used to. He worked very hard over the years through therapy and church to learn to quell his anger.

That was another lesson for me, we can change if we work hard enough at it.

Witnessing him operate with soft power was the biggest lesson of all. My father was more hard power. He commanded respect, and if he didn't get it, he could lash out.

Tom was the exact opposite when I met him. He operated differently and was still highly successful. It taught me there was more than one way to go through life while still being very successful as well as respected.

Neither my father nor my father-in-law was right or wrong in their approach; their differences gave me perspective and appreciation for both.

You might be wondering how this man I'm describing got to the point of taking his own life. I can tell you it's almost never the people you suspect.

Tom, as faithful as he was to God and God's Word, as kind and loving as he was to everyone around him, suffered from a mental illness, one he battled most of his life.

He overcame all of the ups and downs of being an entrepreneur, beat cancer in 2008, and faced numerous other challenges along the way, but he couldn't shake the dark clouds in his head.

In late 2017, a bad business deal left him spiraling. He started another offshoot of his business, one that was supposed to create more stability in his cash flow and send him into retirement.

That's not what happened. He partnered with a young guy out of Texas. Tom was the money, and the other guy was the deal maker for leasing the trailers. Tom spoke very highly of this younger guy (who was my age). He felt like a mentor to him and was treating him like the son he never had.

Unfortunately, this guy didn't repay the favor of the partnership. He was essentially running a Ponzi scheme on Tom. Robbing Peter to pay Paul. He was using Tom and Tom's money to get himself out of trouble with other debts he had accrued.

This exacerbated Tom's anxiety and depression. On top of that, banks were now breathing down his neck even though Tom had never missed a payment to them in 30 years.

My friend Tom Farley (the late Chris Farley's older brother) described the moments before suicide like this, and it has never left my memory: "It's like being in a burning building, smoke and fire everywhere around you. You're panicking, and every fiber of your being knows you need to escape. All of a sudden, through the smoke, you see a door appear. It's the only way out. Only that door and that way out is to take your own life before the fire consumes you."

I need to make this statement before moving on.

This is NOT the way!

If you are struggling with your brain health. If you've ever had thoughts of taking your own life. If you think the world and your family would be better off without you. You're wrong!

That is the enemy telling you lies.

Your pain will transfer to all those who love you!

My mother-in-law, my wife, my sister-in-law, and all of us who loved Tom so dearly now deal with the pain of his untimely death. His pain transferred to us, and I know that's not what he wanted.

It is not his fault either. He was not himself in those last moments. The enemy consumed him. That same enemy can consume any of us if we're not careful.

The most righteous man I've ever known got consumed by the enemy. Tom was the closest example walking this earth to Jesus that I ever saw, and he lost the battle, but not the war.

Judas (one of the 12 disciples) betrayed Jesus for 30 silver coins. He lost the battle, but Jesus won the war.

Some of the best years of my life were the eleven years I got to spend on this earth with Tom. I know that he is in Heaven and that I will be with him again, but not yet.

As we move into Bridge number one, know that this Bridge was heavily influenced by Tom and how he chose to live his life. Every word of it will be to honor him and his influence on me.

The Spirit Within

If you've been in the presence of a living being and also a deceased being, you know there is a spirit that dwells in us while we're living.

Once we take our final breath, our spirit, our soul goes someplace else.

What was once a vibrant, living being is now a lifeless body.

If you haven't experienced the loss of a beloved human yet, perhaps you've lost a beloved pet, and you know what I'm talking about.

I grew up in a Christian household. I was taught to believe in Jesus, but that doesn't mean I just fell in line. One of my most frustrating traits that my parents had to bear the brunt of is that I'm fiercely independent, and I don't deal well with authority.

I questioned everything.

I was on my own journey in faith, and I eventually concluded that I would accept Christ as my Lord and Savior somewhere in my teens. I've been on a journey with my faith and spirituality since then. There have been many ups and downs along the way, but I continue to grow my spiritual being and grow closer to Jesus every day.

The conclusion I came to was that we were so beautifully and uniquely designed that we couldn't be an accident.

The Big Bang theory couldn't have created all living things so differently and intricately from one singular atom. It never happened before that instance, and it hasn't happened since. That theory also doesn't allow for an answer to how we humans were born with this sense of morality, a sense of good and evil.

I'm not here to tell you I'm right and you're wrong. What I am here to say is that believing in a power or something greater than you takes humility. Most atheists or agnostics I know lack that humility and are quite arrogant in their "knowledge."

I was once having a conversation with an acquaintance of mine who is a professed atheist. We had a good back-and-forth on what we both believed to be true. I've found myself able to hold space for others without compromising my own beliefs.

At the end of that conversation, I said these words, "At the end of the day, if you're right and I'm wrong, then we both end up in the ground in the same spot, and neither is worse for wear. However, if I'm right and you're wrong . . . you're screwed! I'm eternally with our Creator in Heaven, and you're in Hell, separate from God."

I am not in any way trying to convince anyone I am right. Your walk with God is your walk with God.

That being said, I don't ever want to look back (if I am right) and have someone I care about say, "Why didn't you tell me?"

I want all of those I love and care for to spend eternity with God and with me.

In Matthew 19:26, Jesus said, "With man this is impossible, but with God all things are possible."

I believe that being whole in your spirit is the first Bridge we need to cross. Knowing what we believe. Knowing what we stand for. Knowing who we are, and more importantly, whose we are.

One of the most powerful prayers I've ever read is known as the "Serenity Prayer."

> God, grant me the serenity to accept the things I cannot change,
> Courage to change the things I can,
> And wisdom to know the difference.
>
> Living one day at a time,
> Enjoying one moment at a time,
> Accepting hardships as the pathway to peace,
> Taking, as He did, this sinful world
> As it is, not as I would have it.
>
> Trusting that He will make all things right
> If I surrender to His will.
>
> That I may be reasonably happy in this life
> And supremely happy with Him forever in the next!
>
> Amen[1]

Most of you probably know this prayer as it has become synonymous with AA (Alcoholics Anonymous), but believe it or not, AA did not exist when this prayer was written. Also, in AA, usually only the first paragraph of the prayer is recited, but the whole prayer is filled with spiritual gold. This prayer is so powerful! There is so much wisdom in those words.

You see, Jesus says it in John 17:16-18: we are in this world, but we are NOT of this world!

Do you follow what He's saying there?

We are His, on a temporary assignment in this world, at this very specific moment in history, and for a specific purpose! One of those purposes is to spread the word about Him, a purpose that cannot be overstated.

Secondly, it's a more ambiguous and mysterious mission because it lies within each of us, and it's up to each of us to dig deep and determine what IT is.

The Bible states very clearly that we were made in His image. When most read that, they think in His likeness or in human form. This is true, but what is also true is we're made in His characteristics.

If God is love, what are we?
LOVE!

If God is infinite power, what are we?
POWER!

Now, I don't believe we have infinite powers like Him (otherwise, I'd be teleporting all over the world on a daily basis), but I do know we were endowed with infinite depths to the very specific gifts we were given.

The problem is that most of us only scratch the surface of those very specific gifts that dwell inside of us. Most of us are complacent and lazy in our beliefs, and therefore, our unique gifts lie dormant.

The Bible is very clear on complacency. God does not want any of us to be lukewarm in our faith.

"I know your deeds, that you are neither cold nor hot. I wish you were either one or the other! So, because you are lukewarm—neither hot nor cold—I am about to spit you out of my mouth." (Revelation 3:15-16)

Woah! God was very blunt in His wording there.

He wants us ALL-IN or ALL-OUT.

He wants us to have a burning passion for Him because He has a burning passion for us.

One of the hardest concepts for parents to understand is that He loves us more than we love our own children. Love is about being ALL-IN. It's giving everything. It's giving all of you to another.

There's a brilliant short book by Al Ritter called *The 100/0 Principle*.

Most of us think of our key relationships as a 50/50 proposition. As in, you give 50 percent, and I give 50 percent. The problem in that model lies in expectations and measurements.

We expect the other person to pull their weight, and we often measure our perceived percentage versus theirs. It sets the relationship up for failure.

Often, our unspoken expectations go unmet, and we are constantly measuring the other person's contributions.

Al proposes a different model: 100/0.

Meaning that we give 100 percent and take 100 percent authentic responsibility for the relationship, and as we do so, the other person chooses to take responsibility as well. Consequently, the 100/0 relationship quickly transforms into something approaching 100/100.

I love Al Ritter's premise.

I've caught myself measuring deposits and withdrawals in relationships in my life. I'm a giver, and sometimes, I get taken advantage of, but that doesn't mean that because I get burned by one person, I shouldn't continue giving to others.

God is always giving us His 100 percent, and yet we don't even leave space on our calendars for Him. If we're sincerely trying to emulate the greatest leader to ever live, Jesus, then we should apply the 100/0 principle in all of our relationships.

Too often in life, we're giving all of ourselves to our jobs, our spouses, our kids, our hobbies, our addictions, our anything, and everything other than HIM.

In fact, many of those things listed above could be considered "idols." The Bible has about one hundred verses that warn us of putting idols above God.

"You shall have no other gods before me" (Exodus 20:3).

"Those who pay regard to vain idols forsake their hope of steadfast love" (Jonah 2:8).

I am guilty of putting earthly things above God. I'm guilty of putting sports, my career, money, my title or position, my wife, my children, my laziness, my ambition, and so much more above God.

I'm guessing you've put a good number of those things above God as well. God will correct you. Sometimes, that correction will come at the most unexpected time, and sometimes, it will be far more painful than you could've imagined.

Take a moment and explore where your time and attention are devoted. How much time are you intentionally spending pursuing and building a deeper relationship with God?

I'm betting, for most of us, it's not enough.

By comparison, how much do you know about God versus your favorite athlete, celebrity, musician, or artist?

I know many people who can name Lebron's stats and accolades more than they could quote a Bible verse. I know many people who can recite every Taylor Swift lyric but not 1 Corinthians.

The Romans gave their people the Colosseum spectacle to keep them distracted from their true purpose. The Greeks gave their people the Olympic Games. In modern day, we have college sports, pro sports, music, TV, movies, theatre, media, social media . . . the list goes on and on. That's not even to mention the identity politics we've gotten trapped in nowadays.

Distraction is the ultimate tool of the enemy!

It seems that more and more, we're all picking teams and sides. We put all our energy and effort into the love of the Green Bay Packers or the Chicago Bears. I'm a long-suffering Chicago Bears fan who lives in Wisconsin, so I know this rivalry intimately well.

We also place our identities in being either a progressive liberal or a conservative republican.

This isn't healthy for our minds or our spirits. This isn't God's way. It's the way of the enemy.

> *The greatest trick the devil ever pulled was convincing the world he didn't exist.*
>
> Charles Baudelaire

I'm not here to tell you that sports or entertainment are inherently evil.

I love football. I love sports and competition. I find great joy in rooting for the Wisconsin Badgers and my favorite pro teams as well.

I just don't let their wins or losses define who I am or my mood, nor do I let their happenings distract me from my greater purpose.

We reside in the great state of Wisconsin. Green Bay Packer territory (not my favorite pro team . . . did I mention that?). Studies done on work productivity, the Monday following a Packer loss, show a considerable drop in work productivity.

We've all seen videos on the internet of a rabid fan smashing their TV after a loss. It's shocking to see grown adults be that consumed and emotionally triggered by an outcome they had ZERO control over.

When we allow our moods, emotions, and actions to be controlled by external idols, then we're playing right into the hands of the enemy.

Have a favorite team, but don't root your identity in them. Have a favorite artist or celebrity, but don't idolize them. Admire greatness, but don't forget that you have greatness inside of you waiting to be unleashed!

You have the Holy Spirit inside of you! That's how I know you have greatness inside of you. The Spirit of God dwells within your body, coursing through your veins inside of your DNA as you read these words in this very moment.

Do you realize this fact? Do you know how special you are?

If you truly did, you wouldn't be wasting your time on things you can't control, like football games you aren't in or Hollywood gossip you aren't part of, like it is somehow relevant in the grand scheme of things.

God is not just some esoteric being living in the clouds or waiting for you in Heaven. He's everywhere and in everything . . . AND that includes within you!

I'm here to tell you that until you get right with God, pursue a loving relationship with Him, and study His Word, you can not be the person He uniquely created you to be. You won't come anywhere close without Him and His guidance.

When we tap into our spiritual being, we begin to discover our unique abilities. And once we discover those unique abilities and gifts, we can give them back to the world!

We were meant to be a blessing to others. You can only be a true blessing when you're operating on a higher vibrational frequency.

It is upon all of us to tap in. Tap into our greatness, our uniqueness, and our giftedness, and turn that over to the world.

One of my favorite poems of all time illustrates this beautifully:

"Our Deepest Fear"
by Marianne Williamson

Our deepest fear is not that we are inadequate.
Our deepest fear is that we are powerful beyond measure.
It is our light, not our darkness that most frightens us.
We ask ourselves, Who am I to be brilliant, gorgeous, talented, fabulous?

Actually, who are you not to be? You are a child of God.
Your playing small does not serve the world.
There is nothing enlightened about shrinking so that other people won't feel insecure around you.
We are all meant to shine, as children do.
We were born to make manifest the glory of God that is within us.
It's not just in some of us; it's in everyone.
And as we let our own light shine, we unconsciously give other people permission to do the same.
As we are liberated from our own fear, our presence automatically liberates others.[2]

You are a light in the world. You are meant to shine. As you do, you empower others to do the same.

This is leadership. This is leading by example.

Only by becoming spiritually whole is this possible. As we become whole with our spiritual being and stand firmly in what we believe, we can then begin to cross the other Bridges necessary to live a fulfilled life.

CHAPTER 14

The How of the Spiritual Bridge

Hopefully, by this point, I've convinced you how crucial our spiritual lives are to our overall well-being.

For some reading, you might be further ahead of me on my spiritual journey, and for others, you might be just getting started. No matter where we're at on our journey, there is always room to grow.

For those who don't even know where to begin, I wanted to leave some notes for you, and perhaps there's something that I'm doing or have done that will resonate with everyone.

Mentors

Who do you look up to?

Those whom we look up to in life have many things to teach us.

If we were to focus just on The Spiritual Bridge for a moment, think about this . . .

What do the people I look up to have in common when it comes to their spiritual beliefs?

Do most of them believe in Jesus?

Or do they follow more of an energy-frequency type of spirituality?

Have you ever asked the people you look up to about their spiritual beliefs and why they believe the way that they do?

Does that align with my beliefs, or does it challenge me to think differently?

When I was younger, I took a look around at all of the people I looked up to, and most of them had one thing in common: They all believed in and were followers of Jesus.

This didn't make my decision for me in and of itself, but it was a telling sign that people I deeply respected for their wisdom and success had a common theme amongst them.

Books/Podcasts/Debates

All three of these mediums have challenged me to think differently about how I viewed the world.

I'm an avid reader of non-fiction. I listen to over four hundred podcasts per year, and I've watched countless spiritual debates.

Reading allows for new portals in the mind to open up. Nothing you read should be taken as gospel (unless it's the Word of God), but everything you read should help you reflect on what is true for you.

You shouldn't agree with everything you read (including this book), but you should pull specific lessons from what you read to apply appropriately to your life. That is one of the ways we grow.

One of the most powerful life habits you can form is reading ten pages per day of a non-fiction book. Depending on how fast of a reader you are and how dense the content is, you should be able to do that in ten to thirty minutes.

All of us can wake up ten to thirty minutes earlier to build this habit if we have no other time in our day, or perhaps you need to cut out some Netflix time to get it done.

You are the average of the five people
you hang around with most.

—Jim Rohn

You want to change your life? Get reading and listening to amazing books, podcasts, and spiritual debates.

The Word of God

While I could've put this under books, I believe it dictated its own recommendation. If you are a Christian or if you're considering what it's all about, then you must know the Word of God.

This is an area I'm still growing in. I am not good (yet) at memorizing quotes or scripture.

Everything we need to know about how to lead a righteous life is in the Bible.

If you have any deep emotions you can't seem to get any control of, go to the Word of God.

If you're ever doubting yourself or your worth, go to the Word of God.

If you're ever questioning right from wrong, go to the Word of God.

God's Word is true and everlasting. There is so much wisdom.

"'For I know the plans I have for you,' declares the Lord, 'plans to prosper you and not harm you, plans to give you hope and a future'" (Jeremiah 29:11).

In fact, I will go on record to say that the book of Proverbs is the best book on leadership in the history of mankind. Even if you're not a believer, there is so much wisdom on leadership in that book that it will blow you away.

My favorite version of the Bible is John Maxwell's Leadership Bible. I love John's practical wisdom that helps me understand better what God was saying throughout the book. Too many like to take verses out of context nowadays.

Always remember that the Bible was written *for us, not to us*. It was written to our ancestors in a different time for us

Church

I've had many friends turned away from church for a variety of reasons. If you happen to fall into that same camp, hear me out for just a moment.

None of the reasons I've heard from my friends had to do with their belief in God. It was usually a pastor or culture that turned them away from church.

I believe that church deserves a second chance. It is crucially important that you find a church where you not only connect with the leader of the church but also the culture.

I don't like nor would I choose a church that preaches the prosperity gospel. I also don't like, nor would I join, a church that has a culture of guilt and shame.

God's church isn't a building but rather a people.

Going to church is like watering a garden. Hearing God's Word in different ways through different messages or analogies, being around other believers, it's all part of the equation to live a healthy spiritual life.

If you're going to grow in your spiritual life, I believe that tending your garden through church is an important part of the equation.

Where else are you going to randomly run into other people who believe what you believe?

"You will seek me and find me when you seek me with all of your heart" (Jeremiah 29:13).

Bible Study

Want to go deeper?

Get with a group that fits your needs.

When Jenna and I were first married, we sought out a Bible Study for young married couples. It was a great group of young men and women. All of us took turns hosting and leading each week.

Some of those couples moved away, some of us had kids, and our needs evolved. Now, I'm in a group of just men, and Jenna does her own Bible Study as well.

My group is comprised of about fifty entrepreneurial men from around the country, and we are led by an amazing pastor, Anthony Hart, out of Virginia. We call ourselves Warriors for Christ.

We meet weekly to discuss all things life, marriage, parenting, grief, successes, failures, and, of course, the Bible.

One of the most important parts of surrounding yourself with like-minded people is the accountability that comes along with it.

We have a spoken rule in our group: If we see someone slipping in their walk with God, it's incumbent upon one of us to call the person out. Not in a guilt or shame manner, but in a "I love you and respect you too much to see you going down this path" manner.

I cannot emphasize enough finding a group like this for yourself. It can be made of just men, just women, or a mix of the two. You need the support and the accountability in your life.

I do think there are things that men go through that require other men to guide them through it. The same goes for women.

You can have really great friends in your circle to have these deep conversations with, or you can have a great Bible Study that does the same. I believe the pinnacle is both.

CHAPTER 15

The Internal Bridge (Mental Health, Physical Health, Intellectual, and Emotional)

Physical

In August 2016, I was in Las Vegas. My long-time friend, Ben Newman (named one of USA Today's Top Five Mindset and Performance Coaches), had been trying to get me to one of his boot camps for years.

He was finally able to convince me to join him. How did he get me?

Well, it wasn't his rugged good looks, and he didn't strong-arm me with his passion or his amazing sales skills. No, he was far more cunning. He got one of my childhood idols to come speak. None other than Jerry Rice.

I played every sport I possibly could as a kid. I wasn't a great student. I didn't discover that I was ADD until I was twenty-five years old, which explained why I didn't thrive in a traditional classroom setting.

Sports allowed me to thrive. They pushed me to focus, compete, and utilize some of my God-given talents.

Football was my favorite sport of all, and I didn't play formally until my freshman year of high school. I played both ways at the wide receiver position on offense and the safety position on defense.

I had the privilege of growing up in a golden era of wide receivers in the NFL, watching legends like Jerry Rice, Michael Irvin, Andre "Bad Moon" Rison, Cris Carter, Tim Brown, and many others.

But I loved watching Jerry play the most. He didn't attend a top-tier university. He didn't have out-of-this-world measurables (size, speed, etc). In fact, it's reported that his forty-yard dash time was only 4.7 seconds. By comparison, Deion Sanders reported a forty-yard dash time of 4.2 seconds.

I resonated with those facts because I wasn't overly big or fast either. In fact, my best forty-yard dash was 4.65 seconds. I'm six feet flat, and when I entered college, I was only 175 pounds.

What Jerry lacked in physical size and speed, he made up for with an insatiable work ethic and desire to be the best. Those two things were 100 percent in his control and what all of us can control.

As I was growing and trying to become my best self as a wide receiver, I would not only study his on-the-field moves but also his legendary offseason workouts. He didn't have a high-priced personal trainer like most athletes do today. He designed these workouts entirely on his own. Six days a week, he did cardio in the morning and weights in the afternoon. That sounds pretty normal for a professional athlete until you peel the onion back another layer.

The morning cardio session consisted of a five-mile hill workout. He ran a trail all uphill, and on the steepest parts of the ascent, Jerry would run ten forty-meter wind sprints. Nearly any other athlete who attempted this cardio session with Jerry would find themselves vomiting, and the vast majority wouldn't show up for the next day.

Jerry did this day after day to make sure he was always in peak physical condition so that his body could endure the grueling NFL season. This allowed him to play twenty seasons in a sport where the average player doesn't make it to year four. It allowed him to earn ten first-team All-Pro victories, three Super Bowl wins, and nearly every single receiving and scoring record. Almost all of those are still held by him to this day.

So, when Ben asked me to join him in Las Vegas and told me I would not only have the chance to hear one of my childhood idols speak, but also have the chance to shake his hand, I couldn't pass that opportunity up!

My favorite quote from Jerry's talk that day was, "I never understood why someone wouldn't give it 100 percent when it's 100 percent their choice."

Something really profound happened on that trip to Las Vegas, even more so than meeting my childhood idol Jerry Rice.

Let me set the stage: I was in a rooftop pool in the hot summer sun, surrounded by some of the highest performers in the world. All of them were fit, like the newly-crowned UFC Welterweight champion of the world, Tyron Woodley.

I was in a conversation with a couple of others, and I made a comment that made me immediately wish I could pull the words back into my mouth. The comment honestly made my stomach turn.

I pointed to myself and said, "This is what's left of what used to be a high-level athlete."

Puke!

Even as I write these words, it makes me want to throw up! It was one of the most inauthentic statements that I've ever uttered.

I've always been in pretty good shape, but over the two previous years, from 2014 to 2016, I sacrificed my physical health to reach the pinnacle of my career.

Sitting in that pool in 110-degree Las Vegas heat, I had reached the pinnacle of my professional career. In less than two months, I was set to succeed my father as the Managing

Partner of our large Financial Planning firm after having been chosen by a Fortune 100 company over a slew of other extremely talented candidates. I was in the process of buying my father out of the business and sending him off into an amazing, well-earned retirement.

But I had let my physical body and standard slide. That's what didn't sit right in my stomach!

The very next morning, Ben had us do a visioning exercise. I cannot recall the specific question he asked, but I know that most people were envisioning their professional futures, goals, and aspirations.

For me, I couldn't shake that thought from the pool the day before.

I wrote down these words: "I have 3 little girls to walk down the aisle someday. I need to do everything in my power to make that a reality."

Now, I realize that God has the ultimate say in that happening, but my mind was made up that my actions would be different moving forward. I adopted the mentality that I would pray like it all depended on God and act like it all depended on me.

From that moment on, I was going to prioritize my health so that I could do my part to fulfill my dream of walking all three of my girls down the aisle someday.

When I returned home from Vegas, I immediately took action. I reconnected with a guy I used to play football with, who was a personal trainer now, and started going to the gym I'm at today. This wasn't just any gym. I chose a place that has a medical spa as a part of the business. It's a holistic place that treats you internally and externally.

I formed a relationship with my now good friend, Dr. Nestor Rodriguez. Nestor and his wife, Ashley, own this amazing facility, which they named Carbon World Health, here in Madison, WI.

I got a full blood panel done to see what was going on "under the hood." What we found is that my testosterone was very low and my estrogen was a bit high. Most of my other major metrics were normal.

Almost all general practitioners would've looked at my bloodwork and said that I was perfectly healthy.

Not Dr. Rodriguez.

Nestor spoke to me about the true meaning of testosterone in men. My reaction when he first told me that my testosterone was low was something to the effect of, "Doc, my sex drive is just fine."

We recently found out that we were pregnant with our fourth child, a boy, thanks to the Chicago Cubs World Series trip!

Nestor laughed and said, "Yeah, that's how they get you!"

"What do you mean?"

He said, "Well, if you tell the male populace that testosterone majorly affects our energy, they will supplement with energy drinks, other caffeine sources, etc. However, if you tell the male populace that low testosterone affects your sex drive, then you get their attention, and they actually do something about it."

Your general practitioners work with a testosterone range of 250 ng/dL to 800 ng/dL. If your levels are at 251 ng/DL, then your general practitioner won't prescribe you anything. They won't do anything for you until you fall below the baseline.

The problem is that science shows that testosterone doesn't just drive energy or sexual function in us males. It's a leading driver for healthy brain function, bone density, fat distribution and loss, muscle mass and strength, red blood cell production, facial and body hair, and so much more.

In short, testosterone levels are the main hormonal driver of being a healthy man.

My initial levels when tested in 2016 were in the low 200s.

Dr. Rodriguez told me that my body was a Ferrari, but due to my low-T, I was functionally driving a Toyota Prius. He then asked me about my energy levels and how I was feeling on a day-to-day basis.

I said, "Doc, I have three young kids and am soon to have a fourth, along with running an eight-figure company. I'm always tired."

He then recommended that I get on TRT (testosterone replacement therapy) to course-correct my body so that I can start operating like the Ferrari that God made me to be.

That, combined with my new workout regimen, has been a game changer in my physical state, and, more importantly, my mental state.

I've been on this regimen and working out consistently for the last eight years. I can happily report that there have been ZERO negative side effects and LOTS of positive side effects, like increased energy, faster muscle growth, decreased recovery time, AND an increased sex drive (which I thought I didn't need).

I get my blood work done every six months to evaluate what's going on "under the hood" of my new Ferrari.

I'm nearly forty-five years old as I write this, and my forty-five-year-old self looks infinitely better than my twenty-five-year-old self did.

Some say that "ignorance is bliss." I believe that's completely wrong, but at the very least, it's an incomplete statement.

Ignorance is only bliss until your ignorance gets confronted with reality.

For instance, you ignore your blood work and what's going on inside your body until you're faced with the reality of a cancer diagnosis. Once that reality awakens you, you start to question things. What if I had regularly gotten check-ups? What if I consistently got my bloodwork done to determine if there was something off that could've identified it sooner?

Ignorance is bliss, until it's too late to do something meaningful about it.

I refuse to live in ignorance.

I'm humble enough to know what I know, to question what I think I know, and certainly to be aware of what I don't know anything about.

I constantly surround myself with people who are skilled and gifted in their respective crafts. I seek alliances with people who think differently from me so that I can gain perspective on what I think I know.

I seek information to help me form decisions about everything. I don't need 100 percent certainty to act because I don't believe we can be 100 percent certain about much of anything, but I seek information from wise counsel to help form my decision-making process.

Again, pray as if it all depends on God, and act as if it all depends on you.

One of the key alliances I was blessed to forge back in January 2007 was with my now-wife, Jenna. I'll get to more of our story in a future chapter. The reason I bring her up now is because of her nutritional prowess.

Jenna grew up in rural Indiana in a family of entrepreneurs. Nearly her entire immediate family was in the family business or started their own. They began as farmers but transitioned to truck sales.

She and her cousins would all play together, eat junk food, drink soda, and get fed very well by Grandma Ruble. And by "very well," I mean a highly processed, fat-filled diet of country cooking.

Jenna realized in her early teen years, as her body was changing, that she wanted to eat differently so that she could look differently. She took control and started cooking for her family at age 14. That isn't normal and certainly not something that would've been on my radar at that age. She also started working out regularly on top of her extracurriculars: dance and cross-country.

When we first started dating, I was in the process of building my first business and was on a steady diet of Wendy's (the dollar menu, of course), Qdoba, and anything that I could get my hands on that was quick, inexpensive, and filling.

She moved to Madison, and I proposed within six months of us dating, so she changed my diet up real quick! I couldn't be more thankful for her knowledge in being able to turn any recipe into a healthy recipe, and her push for me to become my best physical self. She did this with love, not guilt and shame. She modeled and showed the way.

In fact, in 2012, I was in another "ebb" with my physical health, just after our first child, Ella, was born.

I had gotten home from a long day of work and was resting on the couch, watching something meaningless. She asked me if I wanted to go work out with her, Ella strapped to her chest in a BabyBjörn.

For whatever reason, I decided to get my lazy butt off the couch that evening and go with her.

I snapped this picture that I've used for motivation as well as in talks I've given over the years to large crowds. It was a pivotal moment in my adult life and fitness journey.

I had this profound thought go through my head: "My beautiful wife is working her tail off to get her body back after giving birth to our first child with that child strapped to her chest, no less! What is my excuse?!"

She was modeling and showing me the way like a loving leader does. Jenna has gone on to give natural birth to three more amazing and healthy children. We are so blessed!

In the last few years, she's also gone on to get her master's in nutrition education while raising four young kids. She is truly a daily source of inspiration to me.

You may not have a spouse with the depth of knowledge that mine has as it pertains to nutrition, but there are tremendous resources out there to guide you to a better lifestyle.

Nutrition is a cornerstone for both our physical health and our brain health. Science is starting to put out more and more information regarding the gut and brain connection.

The nutrients or the junk we put in our mouths have a direct correlation to our overall brain health.

Most of us know that to have abdominals that show or to have a great physique in general, 80 percent is from how we feed ourselves, and only 20 percent is the work we put in on our body, but few of us know the gut and brain connection.

Our FDA (Food and Drug Administration) does little to inform or protect us. If you look at some of the ingredients that are allowed in our foods compared to ingredients banned in Europe, you'd start to question everything you've learned to this point in your life.

A very specific example is that of Doritos chips. They are sold in Europe as well, but with several ingredients left out. Why? Because certain ingredients (chemicals and artificial colors) are banned for the protection of European citizens.

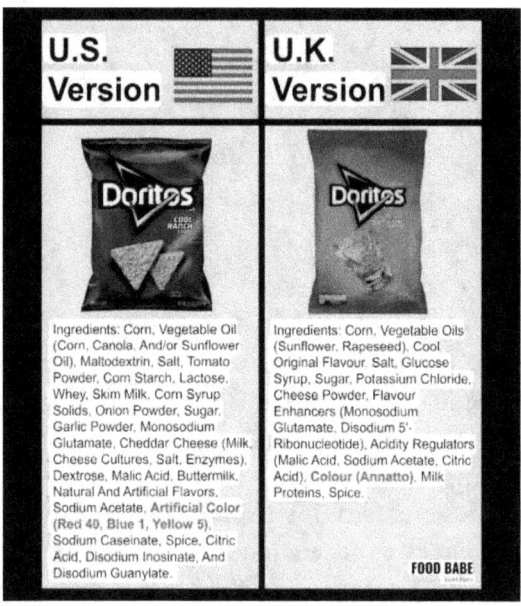

There are many more examples that I could give you, but I'll let you do your own research and come to your own conclusions about why we would allow certain chemicals in our everyday foods here in America.

The food pyramid we were taught in schools nationwide in the 1980s and 90s was brought to you by dairy lobbyists,

NOT because the vast majority of nutritional experts agreed that was the diet we should consume.

What we should've always been eating instead of the food pyramid is meat (particularly red meat), salt (best is Celtic or sea salt), eggs, fruit, fish, vegetables, dairy (if your body allows), healthy fats, and honey.

This is some basic knowledge everyone should have.

We've been lied to about salt. We need salt as our body perspires salt when we sweat. We need sodium to remain in a steady state of hydration. Hydration is important for digestion, energy, sleep, and healthy cognitive function.

We've been lied to about red meat. Grass-fed beef is an amazing source of many nutrients that our ancestors have relied on for thousands of years.

My personal favorite meat is elk. It's leaner than a lot of fish and has amazing nutritional properties. If you can stomach eating the organs, they are extremely nutrient-dense and good for the body.

I would highly suggest getting yourself some chickens if you can. Not only are they cute and goofy, they produce eggs, which have some of the best nutrients you can find in any food. You don't have to worry about them coming from a factory farm, and you don't have to even worry about refrigerating them as long as you eat them within a couple of weeks.

Plant a garden if you can. There's immense satisfaction in growing your own food. You also don't have to worry about what pesticides were used on your fruits and veggies because *you're* the one taking care of your plants.

If you cannot do that, then I suggest you buy organic and still wash them thoroughly when you bring them home. The chemicals used in pesticides have been known to cause cancer. Don't risk your health or your children.

If you can become a beekeeper as well and produce your own honey, then you've got a leg up on the vast majority of society. Having bees on your property that produce the honey right outside your home has benefits in numerous areas of health and longevity. The bees collect pollen from local plants, so the honey produced and consumed has been known to lessen allergies.

And fun fact, there have been studies done that concluded that beekeepers have some of the longest life expectancy in the world because the sound vibration and the buzzing of the bees hit a frequency that has many healing benefits in the body.

We are blessed to have enough land to get chickens, plant a garden, grow fruit trees, and become beekeepers—all of which is extremely rewarding to be able to produce and bring home to the table, knowing where it came from and that it was our love and care that brought it to fruition.

The Bible calls your body a temple for a reason. It's to be treated with the utmost respect and care so that it can last you a lifetime. Taking care of our temple through physical exercise, proper nutrition, and keeping our brain healthy should be one of the highest priorities in our lives.

An example that is appropriate here is when flight attendants tell us to put our oxygen masks on before assisting others. We must be spiritually, physically, emotionally, and mentally healthy in order to give our best to others.

There is ZERO chance you become a Superhuman without prioritizing your health! To achieve BIG goals, you must have BIG energy.

To have BIG energy, you need five critical things daily, according to Dr. Andrew Huberman:

1. Sleep – You must prioritize rest! Our bodies, and especially our minds, need to recover to get our greatest output during our awake hours of the day.
2. Sunlight – Get at least ten minutes as soon as possible after you wake up. That's hard for us early risers

in the winter, but prioritize getting natural light in your eyes before looking at your screens.
3. Movement – Chalk this one in the exercise column. If you aren't into weights or yoga, simply walk!
4. Nutrients – Make sure you're eating for fuel, NOT for fun. Many of us aren't getting the proper nutrients in our bodies simply by not thinking about what we're eating daily.
5. Relationships – Relationships of all kinds matter, but most importantly, the relationships you have with God and yourself!

There are some natural "amplifiers" that help you boost your energy, such as being properly hydrated, cold exposure (cold shower or plunge or cryotherapy), red light, and non-sleep deep rest (meditation, breathing exercises, prayer).

All these things might seem simple to many of you, and I agree, but what's common knowledge isn't always common practice. The point is to execute these tasks daily to best maintain your rechargeable battery.

Who would you be if you were 100 percent in love and secure in your own skin?

***Be careful not to insert society's definition of you in here! I'm talking about you. When you look in the mirror, you are proud of what you see and the work it took for you to look the way you do.

Do you have any idea how powerful that is for your mental game and how that carries into your professional life? How does that carry over into your relationships?

People are magnetically attracted to someone who is 100 percent confident in who they are, not in an egotistical or delusional way, but rather in an authentic way.

I know this is a game changer because I've lived it in cycles in my life. I've been in superb shape, and I've been out of shape and back again. Right now, I'm in the best shape I've been since my early 20s, but I'm not done.

Much like our mental physique. We need to envision our bodies like Michelangelo envisioned the statue of David when he was just working with a block of marble. When asked how he envisioned The David to turn out the way it did from just a block of solid marble, Michelangelo replied, "I created a vision of David in my mind and simply carved away everything that was not David."

Now, I do think that some could take this to an unhealthy level and read into that quote or premise too much. The point is to seek continuous improvement while genuinely loving ourselves. We are either green and growing or ripe and rotting! There is no staying the same!

Unlike Michelangelo, the end date for our improvement is the day God calls us home. Until then, we chisel, we grow, we mold ourselves, all while being 100 percent secure in who we are. In whom God made us to be.

Mental

Are you working harder on yourself than you are on your job?

Some of you may read that question and be confused.

Don't worry, I will explain.

There are several different reasons why this is important for you. I'll start with a quote almost everyone has heard, originally adapted from Ralph Waldo Emerson: "Your health is your wealth."

That quote is hard to argue with. We can't do much of anything if we don't have our health. Hence why it's so important we invest our time and resources into staying in tip-top shape.

How about we add one word into that quote, though: "Your *mental* health is your *mental* wealth!"

Are you doing as good a job investing time and resources in your mental well-being as you are in your physical well-being?

The studies would show that most of America is failing miserably in both categories.

This is why my premise that you should be working harder on yourself than your job is accurate.

Would you like to make yourself indispensable in the workplace?

Would you like to make yourself irresistible to your spouse or future partner?

Would you like to attract the very best talent to your organization?

If you answered yes to any of those questions, then you need to start vibrating at a higher frequency.

You have to remember that we humans are energy.

We are always putting out a vibrational energy. We magnetize or repel not only people but also money, opportunities, business, experiences, and a whole lot more.

We also block good things from happening for us because we hold onto things that aren't for us. Bad relationships block us from finding a good and healthy relationship. Holding onto a past trauma may block us from experiencing all of life to the fullest. Harboring anger or resentment might be blocking you from experiencing true peace and joy in your life.

If we know that, then why wouldn't we be trying to always operate on a higher vibrational frequency?

Answer: We let our brains default back to our old habits and rituals. We let the old records play. We listen to friends who don't know what they're talking about, but they reinforce our feelings, so we feel good.

From the moment we're born up to the present day, we create neuropathways in our brain, and like ruts in a road, those neuropathways get deeper and deeper the more we reinforce them.

We need to consciously break free and create new neuropathways, or ruts, that actually serve us. We have to constantly question our thoughts and even the questions that we ask ourselves.

After all, if we want better answers, we must ask better questions!

When better questions are asked and better answers are received, we can then make decisions that are for the betterment of our present and future. Asking better questions takes practice as well as quiet time.

If you give yourself time to sit in silence (be it with meditation, prayer, or just a walk without anything playing in your ears), you will begin getting downloads from God and the universe.

Those whispers in your mind, those are the downloads. Those are the answers to your questions.

You only receive them when you are still enough to hear them. Downloads don't scream at you . . . they whisper!

Lastly, this might seem obvious, but don't practice what you don't want to become! Change your practice to habits and rituals that serve your present and future, NOT your past.

If you can't win the battle in your mind . . .
You can't win.
The most powerful enemy you will ever face lives inside you.
It knows exactly what to say to you to get you to justify actions that are less than your standard.
It knows what to say to you to get you to settle.
It knows what to say to you to get you to quit when things get hard.
It knows what to say to you that will cost you all of your hopes, dreams, and everything you've ever wanted in your life.
If you can't win that battle . . .
You can't win any of them.

Stay focused on what you really want and never let the enemy within talk you out of it.
Conquer your mind.
Conquer your life.

—Andy Frisella

Intellectual

There's a 1 in 400,000,000,000 chance that any single one of us exists right now. Let's take this miracle of a life that we have and make the best of it!

Our bodies are certainly complex, and our Creator sure knew what He was doing when molding each of us, but the most complex thing He created is our minds. We need to be diligent about feeding our minds and constantly growing our intellect.

The hard truth is, most of you won't hit your goals this year or in life. The reasons are many, but the biggest is that you haven't fixed your "stinkin thinkin" yet.

You are entering this new year with the same thoughts that prevented you from being your very best last year. That's just not going to cut it!

On average, we have around 60,000 thoughts per day. That equates to nearly 22,000,000 thoughts per year. Unfortunately, around 90 percent of our thoughts are repeated. That means nearly 20,000,000 of our 22,000,000 thoughts in a given year are thoughts we've already had and not new learning. That's an astounding statistic!

How do you improve your new thoughts to old thoughts ratio? The ways are numerous, but here are a few to get you started.

- Read non-fiction books daily. Get at least ten pages or half an hour per day. Leaders are Readers!

- Join a Mastermind to surround yourself with other growing people. You are the sum of the books you read and the five people you spend the most time with.
- Seek coaching, therapy, or a mentor. All three serve different purposes and can be extremely effective IF you choose the right one for you AND you commit to the work!
- Take stock of what went wrong this past year. There is no learning without reflection!
- Take time to address some of your deeply-rooted negative beliefs (through therapy, coaching, or otherwise). Mindset is KING!
- Set up your environment personally and professionally to win. Are there friends or family you need to disassociate with? Does your pantry need to be cleaned out of highly processed foods? Do you need to cancel your Netflix subscription?
- Negotiate the price upfront! If you don't negotiate with yourself ahead of time what you're willing to do or give up, you will find yourself negotiating in real-time. Guess who will win when you don't feel motivated that day? More often than not, it is NOT you! If you negotiate up front, then you already had that argument with yourself, and like Nike's famous motto, you . . . Just Do It!
- Commit to DAILY action towards your goals!

If you don't take these steps, you are very unlikely to hit your goals in life. If you do take these steps, the world is yours!

Working on our intellect is more about working on new skills and new ways of thinking.

It's about questioning what we've been taught throughout life and unlearning falsehoods that we previously believed to be true.

Our minds are malleable. We have the ability to create new neural pathways at any given moment.

This is why we must always be learning new things. Getting out of our comfort zones and into the unknown.

As we practice being uncomfortable in the unknown, we learn what our minds and bodies are capable of.

We're preparing ourselves for a future that is unknown.

When you're prepared for anything mentally, spiritually, and strategically, you have increasingly better odds of winning. Intentions matter, but daily action, regardless of how you feel or what you intend to do, will always be better.

Americans *intend* on using their gym membership, but 80 percent of people who join a gym in January will quit within five months, and another 80 percent of gym members do not use their membership more than once per month.

This is a well-known statistic, but I can also verify the numbers because Jenna and I used to own an Anytime Fitness franchise in downtown Madison, WI, and it was the very first business we successfully exited.

Not only is that damaging to their wallets but also to their psyche!

> **You see, every time you don't keep a commitment to yourself, you erode your self-confidence and self-worth. Conversely, every time you make and keep a commitment or promise to yourself, you build foundational layers to your self-confidence and self-worth!**

Keeping our word to ourselves is more important than ever.

Emotional

How do you treat yourself?

Don't just brush this question off! I'm serious . . . how do you treat yourself?

When you look in the mirror, do you love the person staring back at you? Not in an egotistical or self-absorbed type of way. Not in a "yeah, but . . ." kind of way.

I'm talking about the type of way that is so full of love that it spills over into the world. That "smile that lights up a room" type of way. Something pure. Something divine.

The truth is that most of us are still unlearning crap our parents passed down and the world put on us, unpacking traumas, and are completely terrified of being the person God made us to be.

We're afraid that if we really show who we truly are, then no one will accept us. We'll be that seven-year-old kid who was all alone on the playground or picked last for a game.

To have what we really want, you must first become who you really are. The real you!

The you that you don't have to hide parts of for the sake of others.

Relationships begin and end with you. How you speak to yourself is how you'll speak to others. How you treat yourself is how you'll treat others. What you expect from yourself is what you'll come to expect from others.

Here's the crazy but amazing reality. ***Some of you are suffering from self-doubt, while others fear your full potential!***

It's our longing to reclaim who we really are. So seize the moment and step into who you really are. The real you!

That divine miracle that God created us to be.

You are both a work of art and an artist at work.

—Erwin McManus

We let our parents' views of the world corrupt our own. We let crappy friends or social media or any other input diminish our own bright light.

Some might read what I'm saying and accuse me of being selfish for loving myself that much. If that is you, you're not understanding what I'm saying.

You cannot truly love others unconditionally if you don't first love yourself unconditionally!

God's goal for you and me isn't perfection; it's intimacy.

You connect with others through care and love, and you cannot fully love others if you cannot fully love yourself first.

It's time to truly love ourselves so that we can properly love others.

This is the cure to mental health issues.

This is the cure to healing as a nation.

This is the cure to nearly every human issue.

In a world of darkness, be a weapon of righteousness!

Like God is a light for all of us, be the light for yourself so that you can be the lighthouse for others who are experiencing darkness.

Having a strong relationship with ourselves leads us into our next Bridge to cross.

CHAPTER 16

The Relationship Bridge

Every person enters your life for a reason, a season, or a lifetime.

—Unknown

Not all relationships are cut from the same cloth. Every person will play a different role in your life. We have to decide the relationships that are the most important to us and prioritize our time with those that matter most to us. We get ourselves into trouble when we spend more time with relationships that don't matter in the long run and neglect those that matter most.

This is easy to do when your identity is trapped in what you do for a living.

For instance, you can justify spending all day and night chasing clients or new business while neglecting your spouse and kids under the guise of "providing."

You tell yourself you're creating a better life for your loved ones as a justification as to why you can't be home with them.

How do I know?

Because I've been guilty of this very thing.

If we don't prioritize those that matter most to us, we run the risk of losing those relationships.

Let's begin crossing The Relationship Bridge by prioritizing the right relationships first.

Relationship 1: God

The reason we begin here is that this relationship isn't just a reason, a season, or a lifetime relationship but rather an eternal one.

At the beginning of knowing who we are is knowing God and having a personal relationship with our Creator. When we know Him, we begin to know not only who we were created to be but also what He says about us. Then, we begin to realize the Almighty loves us unconditionally and created us in His image, and our Heavenly Creator uniquely designed each of us.

"I have loved you with an everlasting love; I have drawn you with unfailing kindness" (Jeremiah 31:3).

As we learn that He loves us unconditionally, perhaps we can start loving ourselves as well.

Oftentimes, we see Him above us as the Father, which by word connotation makes it as though it's a Father/Son or Father/Daughter relationship, but He also seeks our friendship.

A relationship where we can talk about anything with each other.

A relationship where we can walk side by side, shoulder to shoulder, and have deep conversations about all things.

Walking with God is a Hebrew expression of friendship.

God's goal for us isn't perfection; it's intimacy.

Proverbs 13:20 says, "Walk with the wise and become wise, for a companion of fools suffers harm."

Proverbs 22:24-25 says, "Do not make friends with a hot-tempered person, do not associate with one easily angered, or you may learn their ways and get yourself ensnared."

Friendship is the goal of the gospel! Christians often think it's about forgiveness and salvation, but it is more than this.

Jesus gives all who trust Him the privilege of being His friend.

Eternal life.

He rescued us to forge an intimate relationship with God, who forgives us so that we might share in this fellowship of love forever!

Relationship 2: YOU

At the end of Bridge 2, "The Internal Bridge," I focused heavily on the relationship you have with yourself.

I firmly believe you cannot fully and truly love someone else unless you fully and truly love yourself.

The old saying "you cannot pour from an empty cup" holds true here.

I've had the privilege of coaching some of the highest performers on the planet, and guess what? They all, at times, struggle with their self-worth, impostor syndrome, and fear. We call it "head trash."

So much so that I created a Bible resource list and exercise for anyone who struggles with these same issues. I've included it for your reference as well.

This list is what God thinks and feels about YOU!

You Are Loved and Valued by God

1. **Isaiah 43:4** – *"Since you are precious and honored in my sight, and because I love you, I will give people in exchange for you, nations in exchange for your life."*
2. **Zephaniah 3:17** – *"The Lord your God is with you, the Mighty Warrior who saves. He will take great delight in you; in his love he will no longer rebuke you, but will rejoice over you with singing."*

3. **Jeremiah 31:3** – *"I have loved you with an everlasting love; I have drawn you with unfailing kindness."*
4. **Romans 5:8** – *"But God demonstrates his own love for us in this: While we were still sinners, Christ died for us."*

You Were Created with Purpose

5. **Psalm 139:13-14** – *"For you created my inmost being; you knit me together in my mother's womb. I praise you because I am fearfully and wonderfully made; your works are wonderful, I know that full well."*
6. **Ephesians 2:10** – *"For we are God's handiwork, created in Christ Jesus to do good works, which God prepared in advance for us to do."*
7. **Jeremiah 29:11** – *"For I know the plans I have for you, declares the Lord, plans to prosper you and not to harm you, plans to give you a hope and a future."*

Your Worth Comes from God, Not the World

8. **1 Peter 2:9** – *"But you are a chosen people, a royal priesthood, a holy nation, God's special possession, that you may declare the praises of him who called you out of darkness into his wonderful light."*
9. **Romans 8:37-39** – *"No, in all these things we are more than conquerors through him who loved us. For I am convinced that neither death nor life, neither angels nor demons, neither the present nor the future, nor any powers, neither height nor depth, nor anything else in all creation, will be able to separate us from the love of God that is in Christ Jesus our Lord."*

10. **Isaiah 49:16** – *"See, I have engraved you on the palms of my hands; your walls are ever before me."*

God Strengthens and Helps You

11. **2 Corinthians 12:9-10** – *"But he said to me, 'My grace is sufficient for you, for my power is made perfect in weakness.' Therefore I will boast all the more gladly about my weaknesses, so that Christ's power may rest on me. That is why, for Christ's sake, I delight in weaknesses, in insults, in hardships, in persecutions, in difficulties. For when I am weak, then I am strong."*
12. **Isaiah 41:10** – *"So do not fear, for I am with you; do not be dismayed, for I am your God. I will strengthen you and help you; I will uphold you with my righteous right hand."*
13. **Matthew 10:29-31** – *"Are not two sparrows sold for a penny? Yet not one of them will fall to the ground outside your Father's care. And even the very hairs of your head are all numbered. So don't be afraid; you are worth more than many sparrows."*

You Belong to God and Are His Child

14. **Galatians 4:7** – *"So you are no longer a slave, but God's child; and since you are his child, God has made you also an heir."*
15. **John 1:12** – *"Yet to all who did receive him, to those who believed in his name, he gave the right to become children of God."*

After having them read this, I will ask, "How did it make you feel?"

Often, the answer is, "I feel loved" or "I know who I am and who God made me to be."

The exercise isn't over, though. I then have them write down twenty "wins" they've had over the past year, their definition of a "win," not mine. Lastly, I ask them to write down at least five times they've overcome adversity in their lives.

The whole goal of this exercise is to get them to remember who the heck they are. Once they're done, they feel rejuvenated, whole, or complete. The sense of lack fades away, and they begin to step into their greatness again.

Sometimes, we just need a reminder in our lives. Deep down, we know who we are, and if we do some deep reflection, like this exercise helps with, we begin to remember who the heck we are and what we're capable of.

Self-confidence, self-worth, and self-efficacy come through building a case for yourself that you are who you say you are.

Your case is built every day, or as influencers like to say, "Rent is due, and it's paid daily."

Every single day you are blessed to wake up, you build a case for or against who you tell the world you are. In a world that is so vain and fake, magnified by social media, it is easy to question ourselves and our worth.

Here's the test, though: Can you look at yourself in the mirror and see the same version of you that you post on social media? If I were to follow you around for a day, would I see the values exhibited or the lifestyle lived the way you portray yourself on social media?

The reality is, most cannot look themselves in the mirror and answer those two questions positively. And yet, we all tend to compare ourselves to these fake people because they have a following, and we want that as well.

Here's a dirty little secret they don't want you to know: Most of their followers are bought. Most of the internet traffic is bought. Their fancy cars and private jets are rented, NOT owned. It's an illusion.

When I got into the coaching and speaking space, I told my team that under no circumstances would I buy followers. I don't care what the "marketing gurus" say; that is not me. I want **real** followers who will be impacted by my messages.

I would much rather be an "*impacter*" than an "*influencer*."

That way, I can continue to look myself in the mirror and know I am who I say I am. When I say I'm going to do something, I do it. Being reliable in business and in life is a virtue most hold. No one values an unreliable appliance, person, or business.

How often are you reliable for yourself?

The statistics show most people set New Year's resolutions, and yet, 80 percent fail by February 1.

When you say to yourself that you're going to go to the gym today and don't do it, do you realize that you're eroding your self-worth? If not, I hope that this is your wake-up call. Your self-worth is built and maintained by *you*. That's why it's called "self"-worth.

I don't care if it's as simple and silly as, "I'm going to brush my teeth three times a day." You better make sure you do it because it's what you said you'd do.

What is it for you? In what areas of your life are you not living your true north?

I promise you, living by your values, keeping your word to yourself daily, and showing up for yourself even when you don't want to will forever change your self-confidence, your self-worth, and your self-efficacy.

Having a great relationship with yourself is an inside job. That great relationship with yourself is a lifetime pursuit of bringing out the best in you. When you "settle" with less than you deserve because of comfort, you immediately degrade yourself.

Think of how normalized the "Dad bod" term has become. You can all picture exactly what that term represents in your mind right now: a guy in his 40s who has a beer belly, no muscle definition, and a double chin. He's had to buy a whole new wardrobe to fit his new body, and he's let himself go because he's already married, so there's no point in trying to look good anymore.

And there lies the problem. You mailed it in on yourself and your spouse.

That guy doesn't like what he sees in the mirror. His wife isn't really attracted to him physically anymore. She may love him for who he is, and that is 100 percent virtuous, but settling doesn't serve either party in that relationship.

Then there's the woman who absolutely hates her job and feels like she is missing the best part of her kids' lives, but has settled because they need the money. She feels trapped and is stuck in this guilt and shame cycle with seemingly no way out.

There is always another way.

It requires tough conversations with ourselves and our spouses, hard looks in the mirror, hours of prayer, and hard work to break free.

On the other side of that is the life you were truly meant to live.

Relationship 3: Spouse or Significant Other

The first problem of the Bible wasn't sin but rather Solitude.

God said, "It is not good that the man should be alone."

So, He gave us woman.

She was divinely created not only for companionship but to complement man perfectly and harmoniously.

I believe the second most important decision you will ever make in your life is who you choose to marry. The most important decision, in my opinion, is to accept Jesus as your Lord and Savior. Of the millions of decisions you will make in your life, those two decisions will affect your happiness the most.

Regardless of how you met your spouse. Regardless of whether the relationship started physically and moved to emotional, or vice versa. You work to form a friendship in your relationship.

My wife, Jenna, and I started very intensely and very quickly. I proposed after six months, but we had a long-distance relationship where we spent many hours on the phone (before Skype or FaceTime) getting to know each other and deepening our friendship. There were even times I fell asleep on the phone with her.

She's my best friend. I tell her almost everything.

That being said, I don't subscribe to the idea that you must tell your spouse everything. I think there are many issues unique to men that male friendships need to hash out, and the same for women. That doesn't mean you're deviously keeping secrets from each other. It means there's a time and place for certain conversations to happen.

A spouse is a partner in life. I've seen too many men and women treat marriage like they were just dating and take their vows flippantly, only to divorce shortly after.

When I was interviewing individuals for my financial firm, I would have them bring their spouse (if they had one) in for the last interview. The reason being, I wanted to help them be on the same page and create space for them both to ask questions. They were about to embark on a journey, with one of them taking on the very tough task of making it in the financial world.

I have never seen a supportive spouse make someone's career. That is done by the individual putting in the work. However, I had seen plenty of unsupportive spouses break someone's career.

Marriage is a covenant.

Covenant = a formal, solemn, and binding agreement or a written agreement/promise under seal between two or more parties.[3]

A covenant is not meant to be broken. It's one of the most sacred words in all of human history.

Yet, over 50 percent of marriages end in divorce, for a long list of reasons. Although the studies vary, two show the following information[4][5]:

- **Lack of Communication** – ~50%
- **Infidelity** – ~20–40%
- **Financial Problems** – ~30–40%
- **Lack of Intimacy** – ~15–30%
- **Constant Conflict & Arguing** – ~55%
- **Growing Apart** – ~30%
- **Unrealistic Expectations** – ~20%
- **Lack of Equality** – ~30%
- **Addiction or Substance Abuse** – ~10–25%
- **Domestic Abuse or Toxic Behavior** – ~15–25%

Marriage is hard and rewarding work. Most of the reasons above are not real reasons to get divorced if you take the covenant as seriously as you should.

There are some, like domestic abuse, that are deal breakers for most. I wouldn't want my daughters to ever tolerate a relationship like that. When there is a lack of communication, intimacy, healthy conflict, clear expectations, and equality—and when couples begin to grow apart—it's often a sign that the covenant was not taken seriously by one or both parties.

These are things that could be easily fixed by both adults applying the 100/0 Principle I spoke of earlier, two mature human beings loyally committed to one another, and constantly pursuing a greater love between each other.

To do that takes communication, open and honest dialogue that creates healthy conflict, pursuing intimacy with each other, and growing together instead of apart.

Nothing worthwhile comes easy on this earth, and marriage is no different. Jenna's and my marriage isn't perfect, but it is healthy and loving.

Jenna has been with me when I was just starting out in business, living in a duplex, eating off the Wendy's dollar menu, to growing an eight-figure business. She was with me at the top of the mountain, and she stayed with me when I got kicked down that mountain, only to begin climbing again.

I was her source of strength when she was at her lowest after her father's suicide, and she was my source of strength when I was terminated and my very successful business was ripped away from me, leaving me at my lowest.

Of course, we both leaned heavily on our faith and God's strength throughout, but that extra layer of love, support, and strength from your partner in life gives you so much more.

There are multiple reasons our relationship has worked well over the past eighteen years. I'd be remiss if I didn't share some of them with you all.

Men, always pursue your wife. Never lose that will to chase her and her attention. If you do this right, you'll never lose her!

Remember when you first caught a glimpse of her? You worked up the courage to speak to her, and you pursued her attention. In your courting of your spouse, you sought to impress her, wined her, dined her, and paid her all the attention you could muster.

What if you never stopped doing that? Where would your relationship be?

One of the things I know I've done well in my relationship is that I've always pursued her attention and affection. I believed she was the most beautiful girl in the world when I first saw her, and I still see her that way today.

We communicate well. Very rarely do we argue. Part of this is learning about each other's communication style, and the other part is losing your ego over who is wrong or right.

Very early on in our marriage, we were at my parents' house. My dad and I were having a cigar on their patio while we grilled. Jenna and I were in a very minor argument (I couldn't remember why if I tried). My dad tapped my arm as Jenna went back inside the house and said, "Learn to pick your battles."

It was very sage advice to a newly married man. Not everything is worth arguing over, and sometimes, you may win the battle only to lose the war.

We keep God at the center of our marriage and make sure we're raising our kids with Biblical principles. We don't disagree with each other or override each other's judgment in front of the kids. We want them to see Mom and Dad as a united front, not two people they can try to game.

If Mom says "no," Dad says "no."

All kids will try to play Mom against Dad and vice versa. I sure did! Don't let them. Learn to ask the question, "What did Mom say?"

We stay in shape for each other and our kids. We both work out for multiple reasons. Not only is it a stress relief for both of us, it will also increase our longevity in life, and we continue to strive to be attractive to each other.

We are setting the example for our children in multiple ways by continuing to keep our health a priority for our lives and our marriage.

These are just some of the ways that we've maintained a healthy marriage, and there are plenty more ways that other happily married couples have deployed over the years.

Before we move on, here's a healthy habit that Jenna and I haven't incorporated, but is very wise for couples. Remove the taboo or stigma from couples or marriage counseling. Don't seek marriage counseling when you need it; seek it before you need it. Don't do it as a last resort. Switch to it being a first resort.

We have had many friends do this over the years and have spoken nothing but good things about their experience and how it has helped shape their marriages. We must tend our marriages like we tend a garden. They require constant love and attention. In some seasons, they'll require more than in other seasons.

View the covenant as a lifelong relationship and be there for each other through better or worse.

Relationship 4: Your Kids

Children are a gift from God.

I always wanted kids. Of course, when I was young and naïve, I figured I'd just have boys.

My dad was the oldest of four, three boys and one girl. I was the oldest of four, three boys and one girl. I just figured the pattern would continue.

Jenna and I were always on the same page about kids. We spoke about it very early in our relationship. We both wanted three to four kids, God willing. We waited a few years into our marriage before even considering it.

I remember coming home from the office one evening, and we were in our bedroom. Jenna told me that she had something to show me. I was clueless, perhaps after a long day or because my mind wasn't even there yet, but she came out of the bathroom with a pregnancy test, and sure enough, it was positive.

We were both joyous at that moment!

We weren't ready, and for those without kids yet, you never are.

Luckily, we had about nine months to get ourselves ready. Again, for those without kids, you're not ready when the baby comes either. You get the opportunity to grow and learn together.

We read some baby books. Jenna read the famous *What to Expect When You're Expecting.*

I made room in my calendar to be at most of Jenna's doctor visits. The twenty-week appointment is the important one for those wanting to find out the sex of their child before birth. I left this decision up to Jenna. Though I did want to know if I was going to have a boy, a little "mini me" that I could play catch with someday.

I remember asking the tech what they look for as they scan. She was a veteran in her field and said, "We're looking for a hamburger or a turtle."

I said, "What?"

She went on to tell us that if it's a girl, it'll look more like a hamburger down there, and if it's a boy, it will look like a little turtle head.

I had to laugh. What a great time to insert humor for some anxious, first-time parents.

Well, she found the hamburger, and we were informed that we were having a baby girl.

I wasn't disappointed. I was happy that we had a healthy baby girl and began wrapping my mind around being a girl dad.

Five weeks before our due date, Jenna's mom, Pam, came up for a visit. Jenna and I had just gotten home from a walk around downtown Madison and the Capitol Square to order some food for all of us.

Jenna went upstairs to grab something while Pam and I ate our dinners. She was upstairs for a bit longer than I expected, so I decided to check on her. As I got to the second floor of our town home, I saw some wet spots on the floor and found Jenna in the guest bathroom crying.

Her water broke, and she was terrified.

I knew instantly that my role was to remain calm and get her to the hospital quickly. I called down for Pam's assistance, asked Jenna if she had a bag packed, and quickly got her out the door to the hospital.

Fortunately for us at the time, the hospital she'd be delivering at was only three minutes down the street. Very quickly after that, we were in a birthing suite surrounded by her OB/GYN and a bunch of NICU nurses.

Jenna and I had been big sponsors and supporters of the March of Dimes over the years. We had both heard numerous horror and miracle stories at their galas from families that had premature babies.

Although we were considered in a "safe zone" for our baby girl to make it, these stories weren't far from either of our minds, and we were praying for a healthy delivery for both our baby and Jenna.

In between contractions, Jenna's OB/GYN was prepping us mentally and emotionally for a four-pound baby and what would need to happen post-delivery in the NICU.

After hours of hard labor, our baby girl arrived. She was crying while I got to cut the umbilical cord, a rite of passage for a new father. She was then quickly whisked away by the NICU nurses to get her under light, weigh her, and do a blood test. We both watched helplessly as she was surrounded by four amazing NICU nurses.

Then, I heard one of the nurses loudly say, "Ohh!" I couldn't tell if that was a good "ohh" or a bad "ohh." They wrapped her up and gave her to Mama Bear, AKA Jenna. They informed us that she was a surprising six pounds eleven ounces and was quite healthy for being born five weeks early. It was just her time to enter this world.

There is really nothing in this world that I can compare to holding your child for the first time. I was immediately overcome with emotions when holding our baby girl, Ella, for the first time. She was perfect! And not because she looked just like me. In fact, Jenna said that had she not carried her for eight months, she would've had some questions.

The moment I looked down at my baby girl, I knew I would do anything to protect her and love her wholeheartedly the rest of my life. The moment that little girl looked back at me and smiled, that's the moment that "Daddy's little girl" was made. She instantly had me wrapped around her finger while her tiny hand was wrapped around *my* finger.

A mother gets to carry around the child for nine months (in most cases), building a bond with them before they're even born. For us fathers, it takes holding our child for only an instant for our bond to begin.

My love and admiration for Jenna grew infinitely in that birthing suite. Watching a mother's work as she brought our first child into this world was awe-inspiring. Witnessing what she went through in labor, delivering our baby girl, it grew my belief in God even more. Childbirth and life are a precious miracle.

Ella got her little heel pricked every two hours the first night in the hospital as they continued to check her blood, but fortunately, she didn't have to spend any time in the NICU and was able to stay with Mom and Dad.

The moment you become a parent, your worldview changes. It's no longer about you but rather about caring for another life that was entrusted to you. This precious, helpless, tiny human needs you for everything.

Would you believe it if I told you that our little premie baby was five feet ten by age twelve?

Jenna and I were blessed with two more perfect baby girls after that (Harper and Kensington). God must've really thought I was a great girl dad.

Each of our girls is so different and so unique in their own special ways. It's amazing to see how God uniquely crafts kids that come from the same two sets of DNA.

Being a girl dad was not something that I was prepared for. I had no idea what to expect, but it has been the greatest blessing.

This world is a difficult place for all of us to navigate, but particularly so for young girls.

As their father, I want to prepare them as much as I possibly can.

One of the things that I've done well has been to teach them of their worth and where their worth comes from.

I love to tell my girls how beautiful they are. I want them to always know how much I love them and think of them.

That being said, I don't want them to conform to society's standards of beauty, especially in this vanity-driven world.

Since my girls were barely able to talk, I have asked them just a couple of questions to hammer this point home, and I make them answer me back.

"Where does beautiful come from?"

Their answer, "My heart!"

"And where does your heart come from?"

Their answer, "Jesus!"

Young girls face such immense pressure in this world from a "beauty" standpoint.

I wanted to set the tone and frame the message before the world got to them.

After having three beautiful girls, we didn't know if our family was complete or not. If it was, we were madly in love with each other and our little girls.

Then, one night when Kensington was about one year old, Jenna rolled over in bed and asked me if I thought we were done having kids.

I didn't know if it was a trick question or not, and therefore didn't know how to answer. So, I answered honestly and said, "I think one more."

Luckily, Jenna was on the same page.

I thought my dream of having a boy was over, and I was already prepping my mind to be a girl dad forever. I love my girls, and I'd have a bunch more of them. They're amazing!

That being said, I did feel as if there was a missing piece in our family. A little boy.

In September of 2016, my Chicago Cubs had their best shot in many years to make a World Series run.

In between my heading to Chicago for playoff games and coming back home as I was prepping to succeed my father at the financial firm, Jenna and I managed to conceive baby four.

I was willing to wait until the baby was born to find out the gender. I figured it would be another girl based on our trend. Jenna knew how badly I wanted a boy, so she couldn't wait.

She plotted a surprise reveal for me at my friend Karl's 100-acre property. He fitted a barrel full of chalk and Tanerite while I took aim with my .50 caliber Barrett sniper rifle.

To my surprise, the chalk explosion was blue!

Yes, I fully credit the Cubs and God with the blessing of adding a baby boy to our mix. I tried as hard as possible to name him in honor of the Cubs, but Jenna didn't like any of the players' names. Although Maddon (former Cubs manager) was in the running.

Camden Joshua made his arrival in the summer of 2017, and our family was complete.

April 22nd, 2023, I had the privilege and honor to walk my mother-in-law down the aisle along with my brother-in-law, Elliot. On behalf of her family, we got to hand Pam off to her new husband, Jeff.

After Tom's untimely passing, Pam never thought she'd find love again, nor was she seeking it, but it found her. It was a beautiful wedding with all of her grandkids in attendance to see her smile so big again.

Not only will I cherish this memory, it got me thinking about the future and potentially walking my three girls down the aisle (hopefully a VERY long time from now!)

Historically and in theory, the most important man, usually her father, in the bride's life hands her off to her new most important man.

But what qualifies someone to take that walk and make that handoff?

Is it just being the father of the bride?

Well, certainly not in this instance because Elliot nor I were that.

I bring this up because, as I was reflecting on that weekend on our long drive home, I realized I don't want to be asked by my daughters just because I'm their Dad.

→ I want to be asked by them because I've embodied everything good in a man throughout their lives.
→ I want to be asked because I was the example!
→ I want to be asked because I lived up to the "HERO" moniker.
→ I want to be asked because they're just as proud of me as I am of them.
→ I want to be asked because they couldn't imagine anyone else taking that walk with them.

Don't assume you'll be asked by your daughter just because you signed the birth certificate or played Disney Dad on the weekends.

Work to earn that right every single day!

Our kids don't need a lavish lifestyle to be happy, but they do need us. Too often, we sacrifice time with our kids to get more work done. I've been guilty of this plenty.

We enslave ourselves to work because we feel the need to provide. All the while, we're not even realizing that most workplaces would replace you tomorrow if you died today.

I've been blessed to travel all over the world, and I've seen impoverished youth. What always amazes me is their smiles. They have more joy living in poverty than most of our American children living in luxury.

What does that tell you?

What it tells me is that our kids don't need "things" to be happy. They need love.

As I stated before, love is spelled T.I.M.E.

Our kids need our time, and more than that, they need our attention. It's more about quality time than quantity of time.

Work/life balance doesn't exist only because balance indicates 50/50. Most of the day, we're at work, and they're at school.

Then, as they grow, they have after-school activities and want to be with their friends as well. Your time with them should be special and cherished.

There's a stat out there that sums up parenthood and time with our children.

75 percent of the time we will ever spend with our child in our lifetime is done by the time they're 12 years old, and 95 percent by the time they're 18 years old.

This stat might be confusing to you, but think about your own lives. When you were under your parents' roof, you spent the most time together. Then, you move out to go to college or get a job. Then, you get married and start a family of your own. Sometimes, that is in a different city from your parents, so you're relegated to trips home to see them.

My wife hates it when I state this in front of her because it reminds her of how fast they're growing and how fleeting time really is. It's an eye-opener for any parent. Your time with your children is precious and fleeting.

Our children need us to show up for them. They need us to show that we care about what they care about. For instance, I never in a million years thought that I would become a Dance Dad. Well, all three of our girls love competitive dance.

Do I love dance? No!

Do I love that they love dance and pour their hearts into something they love? YES!

So I show up to every recital and every competition that my girls are a part of. I'll even embarrass myself on stage in a father/daughter dance just to see them smile.

Those are the big things, though. Nearly everyone could and should show up for the big events, but how do you show up at home every night?

Do you show up as your best self for those that matter most to you?

It is hard, and I certainly have been guilty of showing up as a shell of myself some evenings.

You wake up early to get the kids off to school, you work a long, grueling day full of stress, and then you get home wanting to relax, but your kids need your time and attention. They're bouncing off the walls with energy while you're depleted of energy. They're screaming and fighting with each other. There's homework to get done and dinner to be made.

It's a lot. I get it, AND it's what we signed up for when we chose to bring a child into this world.

Here's what I've done to create a clarity break in between my work day and my home life at night: I go to the gym.

I lift heavy things and work out all of my stress from the day. I don't always want to, but I need to. By the time I leave the gym, my mind is rejuvenated, and I'm ready to come home and be Dad.

I've found that my temper isn't as short when I do this. I'm more present in the moment with them. Also, I'm less susceptible to any former bad habits, like eating any processed food or drinking a glass of bourbon.

What clarity break can you create to come home and be the best version of yourself?

You don't have to go to the gym like I do, but you do need something that resets your mind so you can be the best Mom or Dad you're trying to be.

It could be stopping at a park to read a book you're into for fifteen minutes. It could be listening to some of your favorite music on the way home. It could be listening to a sermon from your favorite pastor.

Whatever the clarity break is for you, please take it so that you can reset your mind and spirit to come home and play the role of Hero that your kids see you as.

I have a friend who has a sign he sees the moment he walks through his garage door into his home. It reads: "Your most important job starts now!"

And that is the truth for all of us parents.

Our most important job we'll ever have is raising our kids into being kind, resilient, and contributing humans that will serve this world with loving hearts.

We wouldn't disrespect our day job without the risk of getting fired. We don't have that risk as parents per se, but if we did, we'd take our roles more seriously.

I highly doubt you'd want your kids to eulogize you by saying, "Mom or Dad worked all the time. They were never there for us."

The focus of your life as a parent should be to build a life that you can provide for your family, AND be present for them. When I became a father for the first time, I had someone tell me, "The days are long, and the years are short."

Meaning when you have a newborn, the days will blend together as you're getting very little sleep, but the years will fly by.

Now that we have a teenager, I can fully confirm that quote. The years fly by, and I wish they'd slow down so that I could spend more time with my kids at each stage.

Time won't slow down. I know, I've tried. That being said, we can create memories for ourselves and our kids that last a lifetime.

We hear this term "core memory" tossed around frequently nowadays (especially if you're a parent and have seen Pixar's *Inside Out*), but what does it actually mean?

Core memories are a set of five or so memories that are considered to be the most important in a person's life. Core memories are so significant that they can immediately shape a person's personality, behaviors, and sense of self.

With that definition being so powerful, why aren't we thinking about creating them more often?

Now, some core memories are something we cannot plan for, and not all of them are good.

I have a couple of core memories I wish I could permanently block from my mind, but they shaped me into who I am today.

For the positive side of the creation of core memories, I believe we can be far more intentional.

At the end of each summer, we created a special tradition for our kids, but I will say that it has also become very special for Mom and Dad. Our kids found this movie a few years ago called *Yes Day*. It's a cute movie with a bunch of bad ideas.

The premise was that the parents had to say "yes" to everything the kids asked for that day, or else there was a consequence. It was essentially a bet between the mother and daughter.

My kids, of course, had the idea that we should replicate the idea. At first, I was a hard pass because of the bad ideas in the movie. This happened in 2020, and I know you all remember what was happening at that time.

I felt bad that our kids had their worlds shut down by our government.

I caved and said "yes" to Yes Day! But, I caved with the following guardrails:

1. Geographic – we should remain in one city or area to maximize the day.
2. Experiences over spending – this day is about experiences together as a family, NOT spending money (we gave each kid a $100 budget for expenditure).
3. No ruining Mom and Dad's stuff – you'll understand this better if you watch the movie.
4. Each kid gets a pick on an activity or experience of their choice – in our instance, we have four kids, so they each get a pick.
5. Mom and Dad get one pick in an experience we want with the kids.

This day was a home run, so much so that it has become an annual tradition for our family as one last hoorah to summer before they go back to school. Our kids look forward to it, and so do we! We've created some amazing experiences together as a family.

We only get so many days and years with our kids. I want to maximize every chance I get with them to be an example for them and to create fond memories with them that will last their lifetime.

You can feel free to replicate this idea or create your own core memories for your loved ones. The idea here is for you to become hyper-cognizant of the flecting time we have here on this earth. Your most cherished relationships deserve time, attention, and love!

Be the example that you wish you had when you were growing up.

Be the example you wish your parents had exhibited in a healthy marriage.

Be the example you wish you had in a boss.

Your intention and your actions matter more than you'll ever know!

What core memories are you making with your most important relationships?

Relationship 5: Other Relationships

In 2012, I was asked to join a small group of young leaders when I was still working at my former company. We were all in a similar leadership position at the time.

Although they were called national study groups, in reality, it was a small mastermind. We called our group of six the Grey Geese.

I realize that seems like an odd name. Why not "The Lions" or something really tough?

I thought so as well until I learned about the "7 Leadership Lessons We Can Learn from Geese!", as taught by AJ Recruitment.[6]

1. Geese fly together; they share a common goal and direction.
2. Geese stay in formation, therefore increasing efficiency by 71 percent.
3. Geese rotate roles; they encourage the leader and empower others to lead.
4. Geese are noisy; they recognize and support each other.
5. Geese don't leave another goose behind; if one falls out of formation due to injury or illness, one or two others will stay behind until that goose is healed or deceased.
6. Geese maintain priorities; they stay committed to the team, their core values, and purpose.
7. Geese are disruptive; they challenge the status quo.

These are principles and traits I could get behind, so I am immensely proud of the Grey Geese moniker.

Every other month, we'd hop on a call or Zoom to report our progress both personally and professionally. We also asked for feedback on topics or issues going on in our world.

Once per year, we would fly or drive to a location to do a short retreat together. At this retreat, we would dive deep into our family health, physical health, and business health.

Over the years, we have become like brothers. We give each other tough feedback.

What started as a business growth group quickly transitioned to one where we help each other level up in all aspects of life. These men push me to be a better man of God, a better husband, a better father, and of course, a better leader.

They were there for me at the mountain top when I was appointed Managing Partner, and even more importantly, they were there for me when I was kicked off that mountain top into the pit of despair when that business was ripped away from me.

They've seen me at my best, and they've seen me at my worst. They have never wavered in their love and support for me.

Everyone deserves friends like Adam Cox, Matt Rewasiewicz, Michael Brownlow, Kalvin Grabau-Keele, and Jordan Montgomery.

I will forever be grateful for your friendship, your example, and your leadership.

God created us to be communal beings.

We do not thrive and grow alone but rather experience an absence of both dynamic faith and growth.

"Above all, love each other deeply, because love covers over a multitude of sins. Offer hospitality to one another without grumbling. Each of you should use whatever gift you have received to serve others, as faithful stewards of God's grace in its various forms" (Peter 4:8-10).

We are not just individuals but part of the Body of Christ. Think of us all as tiny little puzzle pieces that form the Body of Christ when put together.

Proverbs warns that the one who isolates himself breaks out against all sound judgment. By all human measures, isolation is a very bad thing! Hence, we can never allow the COVID tyranny we incurred for two whole years to happen again.

You'll notice friends who are struggling with their brain health will distance and isolate themselves from you or the friend group. That's when you need to step up as a friend and rally others around that person. Proverbs again teaches us to never forsake our friends! It warns us of the fickleness of fair-weather friends.

Here's the harsh reality: MOST OF YOUR FRIENDS ARE NOT REALLY YOUR FRIENDS.

They're just along for the ride.

They're there when it's convenient or fun or because you're successful and have something to offer them. They may feel they gain notoriety by your notoriety, especially if you're a leader.

One of the many blessings I received in being knocked off the mountain top after I was fired and my company taken from me was that I got a reality check of who was a real friend and who wasn't. The reality of being at the top of the mountain is that some people wanted a relationship with me because of what I could do for them, not because they really wanted to be my friend.

Some people are only friends with you because of what you can provide them. If you're the boss, they may think being friendly with you will benefit their career.

Your real friends are there for you when you have nothing to offer them.

Your real friends are there for you when you're so in the pits that you're kind of a drag to be around.

They refuse to let you stay in the pit of despair!

They get you the help you need if it's not something they can provide. They speak truth into your life, your doubts, and your insecurities. They bring and give their time, talent, and treasure to your doorstep (literally and figuratively).

Your job is not only to be that friend for them and others, but also to cherish and nurture those relationships with every bit of you.

Remember, the Bible says never to forsake them. True friendship is more like a covenant than a contract.

"Iron sharpens iron, so one man sharpens another" (Proverbs 27:17).

I only want friends who will defend me and my name in rooms I'm not in, and so should you. Conversely, I only want friends who, when in the same room with me, hold me accountable to my highest self.

You know who's not a real friend? The friend who tells you everything is okay and that you're perfect the way you are. That "friend" is fake.

They want you to stay the same for their own comfort! Their own selfish reasons. They don't want you to change because it might shatter their worldview, and they also might have to confront some harsh realities that they're not living up to their own potential.

A real friend tells you what you need to hear, NOT what you want to hear!

Oftentimes, our friends or those closest to us will see things in us that we don't yet see in ourselves. They encourage us. When we have that mustard seed of an idea, they're the first to believe in us and tell us to go for it!

For you to get what you truly want in life, you must first become who you really are. The real, unapologetic, uniquely anointed by God . . . YOU! The you that you don't have to hide parts of for the sake of others.

You might be wondering how you gain great friendships in your life, especially if you haven't had many great relationships in the past.

First, be a great friend. Be of value. Be reliable and trustworthy. Be a source of inspiration.

Second, ask yourself this incredible question as it pertains to all of the relationships in your life: Do they make me a better person, or do they make me want to be a better version of my current self? In other words, do they inspire me?

If everyone asked themselves that question often about the relationships in their lives, I am 100 percent convinced that more people would lead happier and more fulfilled lives.

The Greeks have this great word, **Meraki**. It means to leave a piece of yourself behind, to do just a little bit more, to love, to serve, to care.

We can make others better, or we can seek to fulfill our own needs. Seek win/win in all things! Never splitting the difference is a selfish and scarcity mentality when it comes to relationships.

As we've already talked about, I prefer the "100/0 Principle"—give 100 percent of yourself and expect nothing in return. I'll give you a hint: you'll almost always get more in return than you're giving when you lead your life by this principle. You connect with people through love and care.

Connection is required in our daily lives with God, our spouse, our children, our friends, co-workers, employees, referral partners ... I could go on and on.

Focus on connection through love and care, and see your joy in life grow exponentially!

CHAPTER 17

The Environment Bridge (Professional, Financial, Creative, Adventure, Material)

I already talked about how we should focus on the "who" someone is and not "what" they do.

After growing up being asked what we want to do, we embark on our professional careers somewhere between the ages of eighteen and twenty-four and begin to "figure" life out.

We seek jobs that pay us well and promotions that pay us more. Our parents are proud of us for beginning to navigate the world as adults, or maybe they're just happy we're finally off their payroll.

We get sucked into the professional world of meeting deadlines, taking on more work from supervisors, and hitting goals. Soon enough, our career consumes us.

Sure, we might get married (although many put this off for the sake of their career). We might even choose to have children.

But work, our job, is our driver for all things. We become slaves to the matrix.

Not only do we get trapped, we form our identities around our careers.

We say things like:
"I am an entrepreneur."
"I am a doctor."
"I am a lawyer."

That is NOT who we are, and the more we tell ourselves that, the more we believe it. As I stated earlier in this book, I fell into the trap of identifying with my career and title. Don't let a fall of your own be your wake-up call.

Please utilize what you've learned in this book to know that you are so much more than your job.

The reason we must cross several Bridges prior to me saying a word about professional endeavors is not only because they are more important in the grand scheme of life, but also, science tells us that over the long run, the real reason you fail to stick with habits is that your self-image gets in the way.

James Clear, who wrote the incredible book *Atomic Habits*, describes the environment as "the invisible hand that shapes human behavior." He goes on to state that "we tend to believe our habits are a product of our motivation, talent, and effort. Certainly, these qualities matter. But the surprising thing is, especially over a long period, your personal characteristics tend to get overpowered by your environment."

Winners often win because their environment makes winning easier! There are a number of ways to define "environment," and in crossing this bridge, we'll focus on a handful of key areas I've found are foundational in living your best life.

Professional

What you choose to do for your profession will dictate a large portion of your happiness in life, much like who you choose to marry. So you better choose wisely!

Most of us choose our first career based on our environment after seeing one of our parents or elders do that profession. Others choose their first based on their chosen major in college.

If you choose the wrong career at first, and most of us do, don't be afraid to move on quickly. Give maximum effort and don't burn any bridges, of course, but don't be afraid to move on to something that might be right for you when you know the current spot isn't right for you.

If we're going to spend at least eight hours per day (and for us entrepreneurs, it's a helluva lot more than that) in our chosen professions, then we better work to find one that brings us joy and aligns with our unique God-given gifts.

You won't always know what those gifts and unique abilities are right away, but pay attention. They will begin to surface, and as you keep taking action towards your goals and dreams, they will become more and more clear!

I could get into so much on your professional environment that it would take far too much space. For the sake of brevity, I will cover some really important associations that need to be carefully placed in your environment for optimal professional growth.

Be very intentional about selecting:

1. Mentors
2. Coaches
3. Peers/Competition
4. Masterminds

Study the leaders in your life! Both the good ones and the bad ones. They both have something to teach you.

Seek both challenge and joy in your professional endeavors. If it doesn't challenge you, it won't grow you. Conversely, if you can't find joy in what you're doing, then you'll remove joy from other areas of your life as well.

Whatever you do, do it with passion, and put in the hard work necessary. Others are always watching. You're one connection or relationship away from changing your life.

My point in saying this is that you want to make sure others in your current profession think highly of you, your work ethic, and where you're going in life.

Financial

I was in the financial services industry for a very long time. I still hold some of my licenses, so I cannot give general or specific financial tips that could be deemed as advice.

Isn't it interesting that people like Dave Ramsey and Suze Orman can have huge followings and give advice even though they've never passed a test to give financial advice? I guess the only way to be deemed an expert on TV nowadays is to not be an expert at all.

Anyhow, I digress.

I will be speaking more conceptually in order to help you cross this Bridge because our financial lives dictate how we're able to live our lives.

Money is a tool—nothing more and nothing less.

Money is also an accentuator of a human. If you're a bad person *without* money, you'll be an even worse person *with* money. Conversely, if you're a good person *without* money, you'll be an even better person *with* money.

Money gives you options.

Your ability to forgo "things" in the short term to set yourself up for the long term will dictate a lot of peace in your life.

We live in a world where we are marketed to at every given turn on the TV, our phones, the radio, and even on billboards.

Our eyes are constantly being fought for by companies trying to sell us something. That somehow, our lives will be better with their products. In some instances, that might be true, but we have to know their game.

On top of that, we have social media where we see influencers marketing to us, and our friends seem to always be on vacation.

We see, and we want.

We must want financial peace in our lives more than "things." Forgoing spending money at the bars on the weekends to save for your first home purchase should be a normal thing. Your friends should not make you feel bad for doing so.

Too many Americans have an unhealthy relationship with money. Remember, it's a tool, and to the degree that you can, you should be unemotional with that tool.

Part of the reason we have an unhealthy relationship with money is that we were never taught the proper uses of it. So, on top of being the consummate consumers, we also don't get taught anything about it in our school systems. Couple that with parents who have an unhealthy relationship with money, and we have a recipe for people to spend themselves down a drain that leads to a life of shame and guilt when it comes to finances.

If there's one piece of guidance I can give you, it's this: You must have a savings cushion. It's the most basic financial advice given (and one I can't get in trouble for).

You will incur hardships in your life. It could be the loss of a job, a big medical expense, divorce, or a parent or relative who needs your help. The path to peace through hardships is being financially prepared to endure them.

You need to determine your beliefs about the balance of living for today while preparing for tomorrow. Great financial advisors (as well as mentors) in your life can help you form those beliefs.

Because the vast majority of Americans have an unhealthy relationship with money, you need to be extra careful who you take money advice from.

You will hear plenty of opinions on life insurance from people who don't own enough or any. Those same people will have family members begging for donations on a GoFundMe page when that person unexpectedly passes away.

Work with a real, licensed professional to calculate your exact need and get educated on the different types to form the best fit for you and your family.

Any schmuck at a cocktail party can tell you about the winners they picked recently in the stock market, but I'd prefer to learn from wisdom. I'd prefer to learn from those who have won and lost, people who've made mistakes and learned from them. Those individuals tend to want to pay it forward and give us the game.

Getting wisdom on what to do with the hard-earned money you make is crucial in this game we call life. If you want to lead an easier life and subsequently pass on that wisdom to your children, then learning from others on your journey is key.

Notice that I didn't say "pass on your wealth" to your children. That is entirely personal. However, giving your children wisdom and teaching them the game of money is incumbent upon you as a good parent. Remember, we cannot count on our school system for that.

Lastly, work with a great Estate Planning Attorney to get your affairs in order well before your passing.

There's a hefty list of reasons why that is important, but as it pertains to your kids, don't cause them any more undue heartache by having to fight over assets or decide what they need to sell off to pay for your final expenses.

Creative

What did you enjoy doing as a kid?

I enjoyed coloring and drawing. In fact, I was really good at free-hand drawing countries (very random and unique skill . . . I know). I enjoyed geography, and the shapes of countries intrigued me. I vividly remember drawing Australia in fourth grade. Every nook and cranny on that large island, I drew so that it looked as perfect as it would on a map.

I also used to love building forts with my brothers and friends. We'd steal Dad's hammers and whatever nails and scrap pieces of wood we could find. It would be our hideout. Now, admittedly, it paled in comparison to the *Little Rascals'* hideout, but it was ours, and we used our imaginations to build it with absolutely ZERO knowledge on how to construct anything.

How often do you give yourself the time to be in a creative mode?

My guess for most of you is, seldom or never.

I have lost a lot of that as an adult as well, but as I've become a parent and my kids have grown a bit, I've noticed myself coloring with my kids and finding a ton of enjoyment in it. Maybe you played instruments when you were younger. Perhaps you were a singer, or maybe you enjoyed painting.

Neuroscience has many articles speaking on the importance of neuroplasticity in the brain. Children who play instruments have better brain functions as adults. But scientists go on to tell us that our brains are always malleable; we can create new neuropathways at any age.

That's why it's so crucial for us to have creative outlets as adults as well.

Get off your screens, and get out to your woodshop, into nature, go to a pottery class, go paint, go do something that sets your childhood imagination free!

Adventure

Sticking with our childhood theme: When was the last time you played just to play?

I feel truly blessed to have grown up in an era without the internet and smartphones, a time when we'd play outside in the backyards and streets until the lights came on or Mom called us inside. We spent as much time outside as possible playing, getting grass stains, with dirt under our nails, and not a care in the world.

Life cannot be all work and no play.

Life is an adventure in and of itself, so we need to have our own adventures along the way.

I loved to compete as a child, and I love to compete as an adult. To me, entrepreneurship is a game, and I compete to win in all facets. But that's business and how I earn a living. I wouldn't be leading by example if that were the only place I allowed myself to compete or play.

As I've mentioned, I played college football, and once I was done with that as well as college, I found my way onto highly competitive flag football fields. I've played many more sports throughout my adulthood, and as long as my body allows, that will always be the case.

Now, I compete on golf courses and on pickleball courts. There are plenty of outlets for us to express ourselves and our inner child.

What is it for you?

Where do you play or find adventure?

Do you enjoy traveling to countries you've never been to, experiencing different cultures and foods?

The top regrets of the dying are all around things they *didn't* do, not things they *did* do. So climb that mountain, walk barefoot through a stream, wander in the wilderness, and play games like a careless child!

We only get one chance at life!

Make the ride enjoyable by remembering to play and experience adventures that you can tell your grandkids about someday.

Material

It might surprise you that someone who's spent a large portion of their career helping others save and invest money would include this section in their book.

I enjoy keeping people on their toes!

On one hand, I believe our society has an unhealthy obsession with material things. On the other hand, I believe that some material things bring joy to our lives. The play here is to strike a balance between saving and investing for our futures while enjoying the present. (***A solid financial advisor and financial plan can aid in these efforts!)

None of the material things we buy or invest in can accompany us to Heaven. They will all be left behind for our loved ones to deal with. This is a reality more of us should be cognizant of.

That being said, what "things" bring you joy in the present? This is a very important question.

Marketers are brilliant at making us feel like we're in a "state of lack." They have mastered planting the feeling that we need something. That our lives would be sooo much better if we had whatever they're selling us.

We need to be cognizant of this at all times. Just because our friends have something doesn't mean we're "lesser than" if we don't have it.

When you break down life as a whole, there are very few things we actually need to live our lives. We may *want* a lot of things, but very few things do we actually *need*.

What things bring a smile to your face and joy to your heart?

An example could be a car that just feels like you when you sit in it, or a video game that has some nostalgia for you.

I really enjoy shooting guns. It makes me joyful to plink around with friends at the range. Teaching each other about the tools and experiencing them firsthand just brings smiles to our faces. (I realize this might not be for you, but it's an example of what brings me enjoyment.)

Perhaps for you, it's a Rolex that you want to enjoy now or to pass down to your child after you pass away. (By the way, those have historically shown to be appreciating assets.)

The point of this section is to get your mind thinking about the very few "wants" in your life that bring you joy and to eliminate the mindless consumerism our society wants you to focus on. Some material wants are also great "Vision Board" items that can drive you towards hitting a major goal. Anything that helps motivate you to hit a goal of yours is a very good thing.

Ask yourself the questions above and live a joyful life.

James Clear says in *Atomic Habits,* "Whenever you want to change your behavior, you can simply ask yourself: How can I make it obvious? How can I make it attractive? How can I make it easy? How can I make it satisfying?"

Final Word on Environment

I wanted to put this in the book somewhere because it's an important topic, and I believe it has as much to do with setting up our environment for success as anything else.

We need to celebrate our wins a LOT more than we do!

Before I list the numerous reasons and the why behind my statement above, let me first point out that I used to be awful at celebrating achievements, big and small. I still struggle with it to this day, but I now know the importance, and I'm making a concerted effort to be better.

As they say, admitting you have a problem is the first step to fixing said problem.

We have a comparison problem. We look at others and wonder why they have something we don't. We wonder why they're on vacation and we're not. Jealousy and envy have always been a human condition, since Adam and Eve decided to disobey God anyway.

This comparison problem has been put into hyperdrive with the invention and evolution of social media. Social media was purposely and intently designed to put us in a comparison state.

It was artfully designed to subconsciously manipulate people's identity, desires, and behaviors (not just buying behaviors, but social behaviors).

Billions of dollars are spent every single day to control you. And NOT for the betterment of you or society!

Society has trained us to measure ourselves against our ideals, which, by definition, are unattainable. Goals, conversely, are attainable!

If you've set any goals in your life, you've likely achieved at least one of them. Did you celebrate, though?

A lot of us high achievers don't. I'm as guilty as anyone in this.

Goals expand happiness!

I don't think we set and achieve goals to become happy. We do it because we are happy, and we want to expand our happiness.

If we don't celebrate along the way, we don't expand our happiness; we minimize it. We diminish it. Then, what the heck was the point of setting and achieving the goal in the first place?

In their book *The Gap and the Gain,* Dan Sullivan and Dr. Benjamin Hardy say, "Remember, the future isn't a reality—it's a projection. And because it's not reality, it can't be part of any real measurement of your progress. The only way to measure goals is backwards. Use the reality of where you currently are and measure backward from there to the reality of where you started."[7]

Are you the same person you were five years ago? I sure hope not!

How about five months ago?

That answer might be different, not only because it's a shorter time frame but also because you aren't measuring backwards, OR you aren't counting your wins.

Examples of wins:

- Books read
- Podcasts listened to
- Weight lost
- Muscle gained
- New relationships formed
- Old relationships pruned
- Therapy started
- A new hobby picked up
- A new class started
- A new habit that serves you formed
- A habit that doesn't serve you pruned
- . . . the list goes on and on.

Last year, I took a habit lesson from the book *The Gap and the Gain*: keeping a journal by your bedside. In that journal, before you go to bed, capture three wins from each day. After one month, look back at all the wins. If you stick with that habit for a whole year, imagine the joy you'd feel looking back on 365 days' worth of wins! That would be 1,095 wins in one year!

Well, I can tell you how much joy comes with it from firsthand experience now. In 2024, I recorded 1,119 wins.

When we keep this habit, we aren't measuring against a future ideal but rather seeing daily progress and growth within ourselves. What I found was that they weren't just "wins," there was a lot of gratitude written on those pages.

For example, "I got to see my two oldest daughters (Ella and Harper) compete and win first overall in a dance competition as a duo."

You might not consider that a "win" because it wasn't something I was doing, but you'd be wrong. I was there for them. I got to be there to witness them in their element and their hard work pay off.

Gratitude has been proven by science to rewire our brains in such a positive way. You physiologically cannot feel stressed and blessed at the same exact time. True gratitude is about noticing and appreciating the things around us, especially the small stuff.

When you're too busy finding all the ways to be grateful in your life, you have no time to worry or focus on the stressors in your life. Then, the question becomes, "How long should I celebrate?"

Ultimately, that's up to you to decide the cadence and what feels right. You could celebrate too long and lose momentum. We don't want to take this too far the other way either.

For me, I like the 24-hour rule so that I don't slow down my momentum, and I can continue to progress on my path towards my bigger goals. If it's a celebration for a bigger win, I'll book out the celebration. An example would be a weekend away with the boys or a spa weekend with my wife.

I hope you WIN BIG in your life!

I also hope that my words and existence (however small they might be) in your life inspire you to win.

Just don't forget to enjoy those wins along the way. Otherwise, you'll miss out on some of life's greatest joys, leaving you demotivated or bitter.

CHAPTER 18

The Legacy Bridge (Personal Growth, Character, Unlived Life)

As I said before, legacy isn't what you leave behind, but rather what you leave in people.

We only have one life to live. Our time is so precious here on this earth.

The first funeral I can remember going to was when I was 15 years old. A good friend of mine died in a car accident. I will never forget that day and the pain on his parents' faces. A bright light in this world was extinguished far too soon. All of his hopes and dreams for the future, as well as his parents' hopes and dreams for him, were gone in an instant.

Due to my career as a financial advisor, I dealt with mortality on a daily basis. I personally helped hundreds of families plan for their futures as well as prepare for the worst scenarios through proper financial planning, including life insurance.

Sometimes, those worst-case scenarios happen before you expect them to. I had intimate relationships with my clients, and I was often one of their first calls after an untimely death.

I would do my best to comfort the spouse or family member calling me and assure them that proper planning was done and that they would be okay from a financial standpoint.

I've delivered death claim checks as young as two years old. I delivered death claim checks to a thirty-four-year-old widow with two young children, a twenty-six-year-old's parents, and many more.

Every one of those experiences left a profound impact on me. I got to hear from their loved ones about their grief, the plans they had for the future, and the memories they were preserving in their hearts.

Most of us think about our legacy as far away because we don't believe we'll die for many years. We all know that any moment could be our last, we just don't believe it. Therefore, we don't act in each moment with the intention that we should.

In the world of statistics, there is a glaringly obvious one we tend to ignore. There is a 100 percent mortality rate amongst us humans.

None of us are getting out of this alive.

The truth of the matter is, legacy isn't in some far distant future. We are building our legacy each and every day. Every action we take or don't take is building the story of our lives. Every interaction, every decision, every moment is a part of that story.

One of our primary goals in life is to determine our God-given gifts. Once we determine those gifts, it's our job to determine just how far we can take them and give them back to the world in the service of others.

As Mark Twain said, "The two most important days in your life are the day you are born and the day you find out why."

Each of us was endowed with certain gifts from God.

Don't believe me?

Look at your siblings, or kids if you have them, and study them.

If all came from the same parents, then they were created from the same sets of DNA, yet all are unique in their own ways.

I am amazed at watching my four kids navigate the world. All came from Jenna and me, but all are so uniquely different. Each of them has their own personality, likes, and quirks. As they grow into adulthood, I'm certain they will all choose different paths in life based on their gifts.

One of the greatest gifts you can give yourself is determining what your gifts are and leaning into them.

The great Dan Sullivan (author and founder of Strategic Coach®) uses the term "Unique Ability®."

It is defined by the things that you love to do and what you're uniquely gifted to do. The majority of Americans fall into work that they kind of like and are kind of good at doing.

That is not what Dan Sullivan is referring to. It's the work that you love to do and you're gifted at doing that comprises your unique abilities.

You determine your unique abilities by doing the work. You may have some passion for certain work that allows you to explore aspects of it more deeply. For example, you might be gifted at Excel spreadsheets that let you dive deeper and become an absolute wizard (these people amaze me, as it is not in my skill set).

But do you love that work?

It's the unique combination of love and exceptionalism that determines your unique abilities. These are the gifts that God endowed you with, and it's your obligation to serve the world with them.

It's become popular in the self-development space to talk about an individual's "why." It's their deep and authentic reason as to why they're doing what they're doing. The reason they're waking up each day and something they can lean on when things get tough.

Everyone talks about their "why," and it often stems back to their family if they have one.

I'm sorry, but I think that's a copout! I think that's too simple.

For any of you who have your family as your why, think about how many times you've let them down by not hitting your goals.

If that's your why, then why haven't you smashed every single one of your goals?

If I said to you I'm going to throw your child out the window thirty floors up if you don't hit your stated goal, I bet you'd hit it! But most people don't hit their major goals and therefore are letting their "why" down every time they don't.

Most people don't even get their top daily priorities done, and then they carry guilt and shame home with them. At best, they aren't present for their family, and at worst, they take it out on their family.

Now, you might be thinking . . . well, my family lives a pretty good life or a better life than I had, even if I only hit some of my goals and not all of them.

That might be true, but again, you say your "why" is your family, which means your family is the very purpose you were put on this earth. Why would you only hit some of your goals? Why would you do only some of the things that you said you were going to do?

You say your family is your purpose, but you aren't in the best physical shape.

You say your family is your purpose, but you have an addiction to porn.

You say your family is your purpose, but you haven't spoken to God in months.

You say your family is your purpose, but you haven't taken your wife on her dream vacation.

You say your family is your purpose, but you won't put down your phone when you're home with them.

I had this epiphany not so long ago. I used to accept the family answer from my advisors and employees. I can't do it anymore.

For most, it's bullcrap, and for others, it's the starting line. IT IS THE STARTING LINE FOR ALL OF US!

If you can't get out of bed in the morning for your family, then you don't even belong in the game in the first place!

My premise is this: Your family is the bare minimum. What kind of person would you be if you didn't take care of them? What kind of man or woman would you be if you didn't care enough to do what you needed to do to provide, create a healthy household, and care enough to raise them with the right values?

Your husband or wife bet on YOU. When they said yes, they said yes to all of YOU. All your dreams, all your baggage, all of it!

Do your very best to provide the best lifestyle and environment for them to be happy and healthy.

So when you say your "why" or purpose is family, you wear it as a badge of honor. Nope, that's the baseline! That's the starting block.

You may think you're noble because you say they're your purpose . . . they should be!

I know you'd die for your kids, but tell me, would you live for them?

Now tell me what your God-given purpose is!

Tell me what gifts God gave to you and only you!

What dreams did God put in you and only you?

Let's peel that onion back further. Why are you truly getting out of bed each morning? Go deeper!

If you can't come up with it right now, that's okay. These things can take time, especially for God and the universe to download to you in silence.

Your dreams lie in the whispers. They aren't blared to you through a foghorn.

First, are you taking time to listen? When is your quiet time alone with God in meditation, prayer, or whatever? If you don't have any, you need to create that space.

Ask the question: What do you want me to know today? And then sit in that.

Second, move! Don't sit around and wait for the lightning bolt to strike.

If you're unsure, continue to move in the direction you think you're supposed to go. If and when God determines it's time for a different path, He will course correct you, or He will tell you that there's a different way.

I, for one, thought 100 percent I was on the right track and living into my purpose when I was running my financial firm. I kept moving, I was waking up on fire every day, I was inspiring and impacting people within my firm and in our communities.

Then one morning, on June 16, 2021, God said, "Josh, I have a different path for you, and I need you to trust me."

I cannot tell you how painful that was, but I trusted, and I wouldn't trade my life right now for anything to go back to that.

And remember, I 100 percent thought I was on the right track. I'm living my dream right now. I'm living into my gifts right now.

As we speak, I'm inspiring you all to question yourselves, your own thoughts, to think bigger, to lean into your purpose and God-given gifts.

The vision you get is almost always better and almost always bigger than you envisioned it originally! When thinking about your vision, life, and legacy, it is helpful to know what you stand for and what you stand against.

What do you stand for? That's a great question to start, but it's going further than that. If no one knows you stand for that thing or you don't do anything to advocate for that cause, do you really stand for it?

Let me give you an example: If you say that you're a Christian, could you be found guilty in a court of public opinion or even in a jury of your peers? Would your defense attorney have enough evidence to defend you and your so-called Christian beliefs, or would the prosecution have an easy case?

Ahh . . . this might've been a punch to the gut for some of you.

But seriously, you can't only profess your faith in private. Let's say you read the Bible daily and pray all the time, but only alone.

How would others know your faith?

One of the top commands of the Bible is to bring others to Christ. If you don't share your faith and what you believe about why we're here on this planet, how on earth could you possibly do that?

Answer: You cannot!

Now, let's take this to other things you supposedly stand for. At the end of our lives, people regret far more things they didn't do than what they did. The action they didn't take is their biggest regret.

Therefore, I choose to talk about contentious topics in a respectful manner. I leave room for others' opinions and points of view, but I won't back down or be quiet about mine. Do you?

I firmly believe we are in a war for our nation's soul.

The silent majority and being "politically correct" were a messaging ploy to get us to shut up and stay silent. All the while, the devil, enemy, or however you call evil forces have infiltrated our schools, our media, our social media . . . everything.

So, if we call ourselves good people but don't use our voices in our own ways, how does that affect our kids and the next generation?

The demoralization of America has been taking shape for decades. It's past time for us to stand up for what is right! As goes the quote commonly attributed to Alexander Hamilton, "If you stand for nothing, you'll fall for anything."

I don't think there's ever been a time when that quote rings truer with all the forces we have against us in this social media world and with our attention spans of gnats.

Now, when I get on this topic, I think that most people's minds go to their social media presence and being vocal on social media. And although that is one place you can be vocal, it is not the only place.

In fact, there are plenty of people who only post on social media (a black square or a flag in their profile pic) pretending they care, but who never actually do anything in real life for that cause.

There is a very big difference between virtue signaling and being virtuous. The actions you take are more important than the words you use on social media.

For instance, I stand for kids.

I believe I've lived a very good life, and if I died today, my family and those who love me would be very sad, but I've been blessed to live forty-five good years. I want the children of the future to have that same opportunity!

I've raised over seven figures for childhood cancer research specifically. I've personally donated several hundred thousand to that cause. I've been involved with the Boys & Girls Club and other charities surrounding kids. I will continue to advocate with my voice, my actions, and my pocketbook for our nation's youth.

I stand for mental or brain health. I dedicate my podcast, Spartan Leadership, to the topic every May and continue to tell my family's story to be a voice for those in brain pain.

I co-founded a 501(c)(3), Spartan Valor Foundation. We aim to fundraise for the warriors who fought for us. It is a veteran's mental health initiative to come alongside the foundations doing the real work to help our veterans struggling with PTSD and other brain traumas.

I stand for fitness. With a big impact on brain health, it's a representation of who you are, among many other benefits.

I stand for constant and never-ending improvement. I believe we're supposed to always evolve our thinking and continually dig to see just how deep the gifts God gave us go.

Here are some questions to get you started on your beliefs and what you stand for:

- What do you stand for in your lives?
- What do you stand for in your health (both brain and body)?
- What do you stand for in your community?
- What do you stand for to be patriotic?
- What do you stand for in your home?
- What do you stand for as it pertains to raising children?
- What do you stand for in your faith?
- What do you stand for in your business?

Sometimes, it also helps you clarify what you stand for by defining what you stand against.

What do you stand against?

At the end of your days, what do you want people to say about your life?

When faced with a health scare, it is natural to think about the meaning of life and what your life has meant. If it all ended today, what would your legacy be?

My legacy starts with my kids. Raising four amazing little humans and equipping them to serve in this world is priority number one as it pertains to my legacy, but it doesn't end there.

I want people's lives to be better for having known me. Whether it was one interaction or many, my goal is for them to see their own greatness through me. I strive to help others live better and more fulfilled lives.

Every single day, we are building towards our legacy, with every interaction we have and every action we take.

My legacy mission: "I (Josh) took all of the lessons and gifts the legends have given us and created a repeatable system and playbook to help entrepreneurs, leaders, and influencers build a high-functioning business with a rock star team that they're proud to go to battle with each day."

Do you have a legacy mission? If not, I've just given you an example. Yours could be simpler or more complex, but make it yours and read and act on it daily.

My simpler version: "My dream is to help others achieve their dream."

If you're not taking daily action towards your legacy mission, it's likely because you think you have time.

When asked the biggest mistake you can make in life, Buddha replied, "The biggest mistake you can make is you think you have time."

Time is free, but it's priceless. You can't own it, but you can use it. You can't keep it, but you can spend it. And once it's lost, you can never get it back.

Don't make the mistake of thinking you have time. Don't make the mistake of thinking you'll live until the average age of seventy-nine.

We've all had a loved one die before it was "their time." The truth is, only God knows when our time is up.

You need to question why you were put here on this planet at this exact moment in history. Your life should be leading you to a life of significance. If it is not, you need to dive deep within to figure out what your unique gifts are, the ones God bestowed only on you.

It is my belief that leading a life of fulfillment and significance isn't just a way to live life. It's the only way to live your life!

What do you want said about you at your funeral? How would you be eulogized if you died today? If you don't like the answers, then I suggest you start making some changes.

We only get one shot at this life!

We all can inspire and impact in our own special ways. Our lives have lasting ripples through space and time.

Make the most of yours!

Ready to Discover What's Really Driving Your Life?

You've just explored the 5 Bridges of Kairos. Now, it's time to turn insight into action.

If you're truly committed to living a **fully integrated, purpose-aligned life**—where your faith, mindset, relationships, environment, and legacy all move in harmony—then clarity is your next breakthrough.

That's why I created the Life Quotient Assessment[IP].

This simple but powerful tool reveals how well you're *actually* living across the five bridges:

- Spiritual
- Internal
- Relationships
- Environment
- Legacy

Your personalized scorecard gives you:

- A total **Life Quotient Score**
- A breakdown across each of the 5 Bridges

- A crystal-clear view of where you're strong and where you're drifting
- A starting point for alignment, growth, and next-level purpose

Think of it as your Kairos dashboard. Your mirror, your compass, your call to live on purpose, in rhythm with God's timing, and in integrity with who you were created to become.

Scan the QR code or visit joshkosnick.com/assessment to take the assessment now.

Because what gets **measured** gets **mastered**.
And this moment?
It could be the line between living by default and leading by divine design.

CONCLUSION

When I was at my lowest point, I knew I had a choice.

I could stay down in my pit of despair, or I could choose to rebuild myself and my life.

God showed me not only an everlasting love but also a new way of being.

God showed me that sometimes the worst things that happen *to* us are actually the best things to happen *for* us.

God showed me that there was a purpose in my pain.

It has brought me some of my greatest joy in life to help guide clients across these 5 Bridges.

When I got into coaching, I never wanted to just focus on business, mindset, or performance. There are many of those coaches, and some are very good at what they do.

I've seen too many entrepreneurs and business leaders be highly successful in their businesses but bankrupt morally or spiritually. I've seen too many neglect their health or their relationships with those that should matter most, like their spouse and children.

I've spent the majority of my life around entrepreneurs and business leaders. I come from a family of entrepreneurs, my wife comes from a family of entrepreneurs, and I chose to work with mostly entrepreneurs in my advisory practice. I watched my father work his tail off to lift our family out of poverty, but it came at a price.

When I became an entrepreneur, I wanted to build a life that integrated all the things that I hold near and dear to my heart. There is no such thing as work/life balance, but we can have work/life integration. We will never be perfect in all areas, but we can strive to be a better version of ourselves every single day and to live a life of intention.

When I decided to coach entrepreneurs and business leaders, I made the above my enemy. I decided to go to war against the broken entrepreneur life, where they were titans in business and broken souls outside of business.

I made it my mission to take all the lessons and gifts the legends have given us and create a playbook. The result is a repeatable system for entrepreneurs and leaders to build high-functioning teams they're proud to go to battle with every day. In the end, I want to help them live the life of their dreams outside of their business.

I use my authenticity, drive, and integrity to awaken, inspire, and impact leaders. My goal is to help them imagine, believe, and align their God-given gifts with their vision and development.

I am a guide to help awaken you and your spirit. I am a guide to help you cross these 5 Bridges. I am a *Bridge Builder*.

As your guide, I want you to understand that true wealth isn't just about money. It encompasses your physical health, brain health, relationships, skills, play, and creative ideas.

But more than that, I'm here to remind you: **this is your Kairos moment.**

Kairos isn't just a concept. It's not some mystical idea reserved for the deeply spiritual. It's a divine window. A moment in time when eternity touches earth. A crack in the Chronos clock that says: *Now. Here. You.*

Most people spend their lives trapped in Chronos time—watching the clock, surviving the schedule, reacting to life. But you were not made for survival. You were made for significance.

Never underestimate the power of a single moment because there's an opportunity for that moment to become a profound memory!

Kairos is the sacred now. It's the moment you stop running from your calling. It's the moment you step into who God created you to be—before the world told you who you had to be.

You are not too late.
You are not too broken.
You are not too busy.
You are right on time.

The pain you've endured, the lessons you've lived, the dreams that still wake you up in the night—**they were never random.** They were preparation.
Now, it's your turn.

Cross your Bridges.
Claim your moment.
Live your Kairos.

And may your legacy not be what you leave behind—but what you leave *in* the people whose lives you touch from this moment forward.
"And who knows whether you have not come to the kingdom for such a time as this?" (Esther 4:14, ESV).
Money is finite. Wealth is abundant and infinite. In essence, true wealth and Kairos time operate on the same vibrational frequency.
I won't rest until all entrepreneurs and business leaders know there is a better way. It is *not* necessary to pour our lives into our businesses and leave nothing left for who and what we care about most. Our loved ones don't deserve our scraps while our business world gets the filet mignon!
God called for us to live a purpose-driven life. He called for us to also lead our families, love our neighbors, and pursue our passions.

He called for us to live an integrated life.

Because the time is not someday.
The time is not when you're ready.
The time . . . is now.

If I've awakened your spirit in these pages, please share this book with someone you love. My dream is to help others achieve their dreams!
Legacy isn't what you leave behind. It's what you leave burning in others.

Inspire and Impact,
Josh

ENDNOTES

1. Reinhold Niebuhr, *The Serenity Prayer*, ca. 1943.
2. Marianne Williamson, "Our Deepest Fear," *A Return to Love: Reflections on the Principles of A Course in Miracles* (New York City, New York: Harper Collins, 1992), 190.
3. Merriam-Webster, s.v. "Covenant," *Merriam-Webster.com Dictionary*, accessed May 13, 2025, https://www.merriam-webster.com/dictionary/covenant.
4. Scott S. B. Scott, Galena K. Rhoades, Scott M. Stanley, Elizabeth S. Allen, and Howard J. Markman, "Reasons for Divorce and Recollections of Premarital Intervention: Implications for Improving Relationship Education," *Couple & Family Psychology* 2, no. 2 (2013): 131–45, https://doi.org/10.1037/a0032025.
5. Paul R. Amato and Denise Previti, "People's Reasons for Divorcing: Gender, Social Class, the Life Course, and Adjustment," *Journal of Family Issues* 24, no. 5 (2003): 602–626, https://doi.org/10.1177/0192513X03254507.
6. "7 Leadership Lessons We Can Learn from Geese!," AJ Recruitment, May 25, 2021, https://www.ajrecruitment.com/blog/7-leadership-lessons-we-can-learn-from-geese/.
7. Dan Sullivan and Benjamin Hardy, The Gap and the Gain: The High Achievers Guide to Happiness, Confidence, and Success (Carlsbad, CA: Hay House, Inc, 2021).

ABOUT THE AUTHOR

Josh Kosnick is a Bridge Builder—a leader forged through fire and guided by faith. As the founder of Kairos Coaching and a Professional EOS Implementer®, Josh has dedicated his life to helping individuals and organizations align vision with execution. With firsthand experience building and exiting three successful businesses, he understands what it takes to create sustainable value while navigating the challenges of leadership, growth, and transformation.

Josh's unique journey has positioned him as more than a coach—he's a mentor, a visionary, and a guide. Through his masterminds, coaching programs, and speaking engagements, he empowers others to cross the bridges of struggle and uncertainty to discover purpose, resilience, and fulfillment. He believes leadership isn't about titles or accolades but about fostering meaningful connections, building trust, and leaving a legacy that inspires others.

A passionate advocate for men's mental health, Josh is committed to breaking down barriers around vulnerability, helping others transform pain into purpose. He knows that true strength lies in authenticity and that the most significant breakthroughs often come from the hardest battles. His faith fuels his mission, providing the foundation for his unyielding drive to inspire others to live with intention and impact.

As an EOS Implementer, Josh brings clarity and alignment to teams, helping businesses operate at their highest potential. He blends strategic frameworks with personal insights, guiding leaders to build organizations that are not only profitable but also purpose-driven.

His experience as a business leader and entrepreneur enables him to speak with authority, yet his humility ensures his lessons resonate deeply. Beyond his professional endeavors, Josh is a father of four and a believer in the power of legacy, not as something left behind but as something instilled in others. Whether mentoring through Kairos Coaching, hosting transformational masterminds, or guiding businesses to scale with intention, Josh embodies the ethos of generosity, authenticity, and resilience.

Josh's message is clear: Success is about more than achievements; it's about crossing the bridges that connect your vision to your purpose, transforming adversity into growth, and leaving a lasting impact on the lives you touch.

Inspire Your Audience

BRING JOSH TO YOUR NEXT EVENT

Josh Kosnick delivers keynotes and workshops that challenge, inspire, and equip leaders to align their purpose with their performance. If your audience is ready for a message that moves them to action and deeper clarity, let's connect.

www.joshkosnick.com/speaking

GET A GRIP ON YOUR BUSINESS

WITH THE ENTREPRENEURIAL OPERATING SYSTEM®

EOSWorldWide.com

THE TRACTION LIBRARY™

GETTING EVERYONE IN YOUR COMPANY ON THE SAME PAGE

TRACTION: GET A GRIP ON YOUR BUSINESS
Strengthen the Six Key Components® of your business using simple yet powerful tools and disciplines.

FOR EVERYONE

GET STARTED:

ROCKET FUEL: THE ONE ESSENTIAL COMBINATION
Dive into how the Visionary and Integrator duo can take their company to new heights.
FOR VISIONARIES & INTEGRATORS

GET A GRIP: AN ENTREPRENEURIAL FABLE
Follow this fable's characters as they learn how to run on EOS® and address real-world business situations.
FOR THE LEADERSHIP TEAM

WHAT THE HECK IS EOS?
Create ownership and buy-in from every employee in your organization, inspiring them to take an active role in achieving your company's vision.
FOR ALL EMPLOYEES, MANAGERS, & SUPERVISORS

HOW TO BE A GREAT BOSS!
Help bosses at all levels of your organization get the most from their people.
FOR LEADERS, MANAGERS, & SUPERVISORS

THE EOS LIFE
Learn how to create your ideal life by doing what you love, with people you love, making a huge difference, being compensated appropriately, and with time for other passions.
FOR ENTREPRENEURS & LEADERSHIP TEAMS

THE EOS MASTERY SERIES™
Dive deeper into each of the Six Key Components® for more masterful execution.

EOSWORLDWIDE.COM

THIS BOOK IS PROTECTED INTELLECTUAL PROPERTY

The author of this book values Intellectual Property. The book you just read is protected by Instant IP[IP], a proprietary process, which integrates blockchain technology giving Intellectual Property "Global Protection." By creating a "Time-Stamped" smart contract that can never be tampered with or changed, we establish "First Use" that tracks back to the author.

Instant IP [IP] functions much like a Pre-Patent since it provides an immutable "First Use" of the Intellectual Property. This is achieved through our proprietary process of leveraging blockchain technology and smart contracts. As a result, proving "First Use" is simple through a global and verifiable smart contract. By protecting intellectual property with blockchain technology and smart contracts, we establish a "First to File" event.

Protected by Instant IP [IP]

LEARN MORE AT INSTANTIP.TODAY